MW01039252

COLLECTED WORKS OF RENÉ GUÉNON

THE ESOTERISM OF DANTE

RENÉ GUÉNON

THE
ESOTERISM
OF DANTE

Translators
Henry D. Fohr
Cecil Bethell

Editor
Samuel D. Fohr

SOPHIA PERENNIS

HILLSDALE NY

Originally published in
French as *L'Ésotérisme de Dante*
© Éditions Gallimard 1925, 1957
First English edition © Sophia Perennis 1996
Second, revised English edition © Sophia Perennis 2001
Second Impression 2004

Series editor: James R. Wetmore

For information, address:
Sophia Perennis, P.O. Box 611
Hillsdale NY 12529
sophiaperennis.com

Library of Congress Cataloging-in-Publication Data

Guénon, René
[Ésotérisme de Dante. English]
The esoterism of Dante / René Guénon ; translated by
Henry D. Fohr, Cecil Bethell ; edited by Samuel D. Fohr—2nd, rev. ed.

p. cm. —— (Collected works of René Guénon)
Includes bibliographical references and index.
ISBN 0 900588 64 0 (pbk: alk. paper)
ISBN 0 900588 48 9 (cloth: alk. paper)
1. Dante Alighieri, 1265–1321—Criticism and interpretation 2.
Symbolism of numbers in literature. I. Fohr, S.D., 1943– II. Title.
PQ4407.N8 G813 2001
851'.1—dc21   2001001095

THE PUBLISHER
GIVES SPECIAL THANKS TO
HENRY D. AND JENNIE L. FOHR
FOR MAKING THIS EDITION POSSIBLE

CONTENTS

EDITORIAL NOTE

THE PAST CENTURY HAS WITNESSED an erosion of earlier cultural values as well as a blurring of the distinctive characteristics of the world's traditional civilizations, giving rise to philosophic and moral relativism, multiculturalism, and dangerous fundamentalist reactions. As early as the 1920s, the French metaphysician René Guénon (1886–1951) had diagnosed these tendencies and presented what he believed to be the only possible reconciliation of the legitimate, although apparently conflicting, demands of outward religious forms, 'exoterisms', with their essential core, 'esoterism'. His works are characterized by a foundational critique of the modern world coupled with a call for intellectual reform; a renewed examination of metaphysics, the traditional sciences, and symbolism, with special reference to the ultimate unanimity of all spiritual traditions; and finally, a call to the work of spiritual realization. Despite their wide influence, translation of Guénon's works into English has so far been piecemeal. The *Sophia Perennis* edition is intended to fill the urgent need to present them in a more authoritative and systematic form. A complete list of Guénon's works, given in the order of their original publication in French, follows this note.

In the middle of the nineteenth century two scholars, Gabriele Rossetti and Eugène Aroux, pointed to a deeper level of meaning in Dante's work, notably in *The Divine Comedy*. Although their views were radically opposed on religious and social matters, they shared the view that it was this deeper meaning that had made Dante appear to be both a heretic and a revolutionary. From their theses, which he reviews in the present book, Guénon retains only those elements that place beyond doubt the existence of such a hidden meaning—or rather, hidden meanings—in the writings of the great Florentine; but he also makes clear that esoterism is not the same as 'heresy' and that a doctrine reserved for an elite can be superimposed on the teaching given to the faithful without thereby standing in opposition to it. In the social domain likewise Dante is neither revolutionary nor 'socialist', but deeply traditional. He defends the idea of the Holy Empire, and the separation within Christianity of spiritual authority and temporal power, although they are found united in other traditional forms—a point Guénon returns to in later writings.

In *The Esoterism of Dante*, Guénon undertakes to establish that the three divisions of *The Divine Comedy* represent stages of initiatic realization and testify to Dante's knowledge of traditional sciences unknown to the moderns: the science of numbers, of cosmic cycles, and of sacred astrology. He also touches on the all important question of medieval esoterism, and corrects the errors of earlier scholars who had only glimpsed the deeper meaning of Dante's work—providing an entirely new explanation of numerous points not previously elucidated. Some of the same themes are further developed in Guénon's *Insights into Christian Esoterism* and elsewhere.

Guénon often uses words or expressions set off in 'scare quotes'. To avoid clutter, single quotation marks have been used throughout. As for transliterations, Guénon was more concerned with phonetic fidelity than academic usage. The system adopted here reflects the views of scholars familiar both with the languages and Guénon's writings. Brackets indicate editorial insertions, or, within citations, Guénon's additions. Wherever possible, references have been updated, and English editions substituted.

The present translation is based on the work of Henry D. Fohr, edited by his son Samuel Fohr, and an earlier version done by Cecil Bethell with the help of Jacques Phillipe. The entire text was checked for accuracy and further revised by Marie Hansen. For help with selected chapters and proofreading thanks go to John Riess, John Champoux, John Ahmed Herlihy, and William Quinn. A special debt of thanks is owed to Cecil Bethell, who revised and proofread the text at several stages and provided the index. Cover design by Michael Buchino and Gray Henry, based on a drawing of Christ between two serpents from an ancient Irish motif, by Guénon's friend and collaborator Ananda K. Coomaraswamy.

THE WORKS
OF RENÉ GUÉNON

*Introduction to the Study
of the Hindu Doctrines* (1921)

*Theosophy: History of
a Pseudo-Religion* (1921)

The Spiritist Fallacy (1923)

East and West (1924)

*Man and His Becoming
according to the Vedānta* (1925)

The Esoterism of Dante (1925)

The Crisis of the Modern World
(1927)

The King of the World (1927)

*Spiritual Authority and
Temporal Power* (1929)

The Symbolism of the Cross (1931)

The Multiple States of the Being
(1932)

*The Reign of Quantity and
the Signs of the Times* (1945)

Perspectives on Initiation (1946)

The Great Triad (1946)

*The Metaphysical Principles of
the Infinitesimal Calculus* (1946)

*Initiation and Spiritual
Realization* (1952)

*Insights into Christian
Esoterism* (1954)

Symbols of Sacred Science (1962)

*Studies in Freemasonry
and the Compagnonnage* (1964)

Studies in Hinduism (1966)

*Traditional Forms and Cosmic
Cycles* (1970)

*Insights into Islamic Esoterism
and Taoism* (1973)

Reviews (1973)

Miscellanea (1976)

1

APPARENT AND
HIDDEN MEANING

O voi che avete gl'intelletti sani,
Mirate la dottrina che s'asconde
Sotto il velame delli versi strani!

WITH THESE WORDS[1] Dante indicates quite explicitly that there is a hidden and, properly speaking, doctrinal significance to his work, whose external and apparent meaning is only a veil that must be penetrated by those who would understand it. Elsewhere the poet goes still further, declaring that all writings, and not only sacred ones, can be understood and must be explained principally according to four levels of meaning: *si possono intendere e debbonsi sponere massimamente per quattro sensi.*[2] It is evident moreover that these diverse meanings cannot in any way neutralize or oppose each other, but on the contrary must complete each other, harmonizing

---

1. *Inferno,* IX, 61–63. [All citations from *The Divine Comedy* in the text and appended to notes are taken from John Ciardi's translation (New York: W.W. Norton & Company, Inc., 1977). Emphasis is always Guénon's. In the Ciardi translation, the lines cited here are numbered 58–60. ED.]

> Men of sound intellect and probity,
> Weigh with good understanding what lies hidden
> Behind the veil of my strange allegory!

2. *Convivio,* t. II, chap. I. 'They may be understood, and they must be explained in four senses.'

like the parts within a whole or as constituent elements of one single synthesis.

There is thus no doubt whatsoever that the *Divine Comedy* in its entirety can be interpreted in several senses, for we have in this regard the testimony of its author, who is certainly better qualified than anyone else to inform us of his own intentions. The difficulty begins only when it comes to determining these different meanings, especially the highest or the most profound, and it is here that different points of view naturally arise among commentators. They all generally agree on recognizing beneath the literal meaning in poetic narrative a philosophical (or rather, philosophico-theological) meaning, and also a political and social one; however, counting the literal meaning, this still makes only three, and Dante advises us to look for a fourth meaning. What can it be? For us, it can only be a properly initiatic meaning, metaphysical in its essence, to which are related numerous facts, equally esoteric in character though not all of a purely metaphysical order. It is precisely owing to its esoteric character that this profounder level of meaning has completely escaped most commentators. Yet if one ignores it, or perhaps fails to recognize it, the other levels of meaning can themselves only be partially grasped, for this fourth, or initiatic, meaning stands to the others as their principle, in which their multiplicity is coordinated and unified.

Even those who have glimpsed the esoteric side of Dante's work have committed many mistakes with respect to its true nature, for they have usually lacked a real understanding of these things, and their interpretations have been affected by prejudices that they found impossible to lay aside. Thus it is that Rossetti and Aroux, who were among the first to point out the existence of this esoterism, could conclude that Dante was guilty of 'heresy', not realizing that they were mixing together considerations relating to altogether different domains; so that, although they knew certain things, there were many others they did not know, and which we shall attempt to point out without in any way claiming to give a complete exposition of a subject that indeed seems truly inexhaustible.

The question for Aroux was whether Dante was Catholic or Albigensian. For others it seems rather to be whether he was Christian or pagan.[3] For our part, we do not think that such a point of view is necessary, for true esoterism is something completely different from outward religion, and if it has some relationship with it, this can only be insofar as it finds a symbolic mode of expression in religious forms. Moreover, it matters little whether these forms be of this or that religion, since what is involved is the essential doctrinal unity concealed beneath their apparent diversity. This is why in the past initiates participated in all forms of worship, following the customs established in whatever country they happened to be. Dante also understood this fundamental unity, and for this reason, and not by virtue of any superficial 'syncretism', he employed indifferently a terminology borrowed from Christianity and Greco-Roman antiquity as circumstances required. Pure metaphysics is neither pagan nor Christian, but universal; the ancient mysteries were not paganism, but were superimposed upon it.[4] In the same way there were in the Middle Ages some organizations of an initiatic, and not religious, character, but which took Catholicism as their base. If Dante belonged to some of these organizations, which seems to us indisputable, this is no reason to declare him a 'heretic'. Those who think in this way give proof of a false or incomplete idea of the Middle Ages; they see only the outer aspect of things so to speak, because for all other aspects terms of comparison are no longer to be found in the modern world.

Such being the real character of all initiatic organizations, there were only two cases where an accusation of 'heresy' might have been leveled at some of them, or at least at some of their members, and this in order to conceal other grounds for complaint that were much more legitimate, but which could not be expressed openly. In the first case certain initiates indulged in inopportune disclosures, risking both a disturbance in minds as yet unprepared for knowledge of higher truths, and also provoking disorder at the social level. The

---

3. Cf. Arturo Reghini, 'L'Allegoria esoterica di Dante', in *Nouvo Patto*, September–November 1921, pp541–548.

4. We must say that we would prefer another word to 'paganism', which has been imposed by long usage but was originally only a term of contempt applied to the Greco-Roman religion in the last stage of its decadence, where it was reduced to the state of simple popular 'superstition'.

authors of such disclosures erred in creating a confusion of the esoteric and the exoteric orders, a confusion that sufficiently justified
the reproach of 'heresy'. This situation has arisen on a number of
occasions in Islam,[5] where, however, the esoteric schools do not
normally encounter any hostility at the hand of the religious and
judicial authorities representing exoterism. In the second case, the
same accusation was simply taken as a pretext by a political power to
destroy adversaries thought all the more formidable for being so
difficult to reach by ordinary means. The destruction of the Order of
the Temple is the most celebrated instance of this type, and this
event has a direct connection with the subject of the present study.

5. We make particular allusion to the celebrated example of Al-Ḥallāj, who was
put to death in Baghdad in the year 309 of the Hegira (AD 921), and whose memory
is venerated even by those who think he was justly condemned for his imprudent
disclosures.

2

THE 'FEDE SANTA'

IN THE VIENNA MUSEUM ARE TWO MEDALLIONS, one representing Dante and the other the painter Peter of Pisa; the reverse side of each bear the letters F.S.K.I.P.F.T., which Aroux interprets as: *Frater Sacrae Kadosch, Imperialis Principatus, Frater Templarius.* For the first three letters this interpretation is obviously incorrect and does not convey any intelligible meaning; we think it should read *Fidei Sanctae Kadosch.* The association of the *Fede Santa*, of which Dante seems to have been a leader, was a tertiary order of Templar filiation, justifying the name *Frater Templarius*; and its dignitaries bore the title of *Kadosch*, a Hebrew word meaning 'holy' or 'consecrated', which has been preserved to our days in the high grades of Masonry. It is then not without reason that Dante takes Saint Bernard, who established the rule of the Order of the Temple, as his guide for the completion of his own celestial journey,[1] apparently wishing to point out in this way that, given the conditions characteristic of his time, access to the highest possible degree of the spiritual hierarchy was attainable only in this way.

In order to explain the *Imperialis Principatus*, perhaps one need not limit oneself to considering Dante's political role, which shows that the organizations to which he belonged were at the time well disposed toward the imperial power. We must point out moreover that the 'Holy Empire' has a symbolic significance and that even today in Scottish Masonry the members of the Supreme Councils bear the titles of dignitaries of the Holy Empire, while the title

---

1. *Paradiso*, XXXI. The word *contemplante*, which Dante uses later to describe Saint Bernard (idem, XXXII, 1), appears to have a double meaning due to its affinity with the name of the *Temple* itself.

'Prince' appears in the denominations of many grades. Furthermore, beginning with the sixteenth century the leaders of the different organizations of Rosicrucian origin bore the title of Imperator; and there are reasons to think that in Dante's time the *Fede Santa* bore certain similarities to what later became the 'Brotherhood of the Rose-Cross', even if the latter is not more or less directly derived from the former.

We shall find many more parallels of this kind, and Aroux himself indicated a considerable number of them. One of the essential points on which he shed light, without perhaps drawing from it all the conclusions it implies, is the significance of the different symbolic regions Dante describes, and more especially the 'heavens'. These regions actually represent as many different states, and the heavens are properly speaking 'spiritual hierarchies', that is to say degrees of initiation. In this context an interesting concordance could be established between the conception of Dante and that of Swedenborg, not to speak of certain theories of the Hebrew Kabbalah, and especially of Islamic esoterism. In this regard Dante himself has provided a clue worth mentioning: *A vedere quello che per terzo cielo s'intende . . . dico che per* CIELO *intendo la scienza e per* CIELI *le scienze* [author's emphasis].[2] But what exactly are these 'sciences' understood under the symbolic designation of the 'heavens', and should we see therein an allusion to the 'seven liberal arts' so often mentioned elsewhere by Dante and his contemporaries? What leads us to think that this must be the case is that according to Aroux, 'the Cathars had signs of recognition, passwords, and astrological doctrine as early as the twelfth century; they conducted their initiations at the vernal equinox; their scientific system was founded on the doctrine of correspondences: Grammar corresponded to the Moon, Dialectic to Mercury, Rhetoric to Venus, Music to Mars, Geometry to Jupiter, Astronomy to Saturn, and Arithmetic or Illumined Reason to the Sun.' Accordingly, to the seven planetary spheres—the first seven of Dante's nine heavens—corresponded the seven liberal arts respectively; and precisely these same designations are depicted

---

2. *Convivio*, t.II, chap. 14. 'To see what is meant by this third heaven, I say that by *heaven* I mean science, and by *heavens*, sciences.'

on the seven rungs of the left upright of the *Ladder of the Kadosch* (30th degree of Scottish Masonry). The ascending order, in this latter case, differs only in an inversion, on the one hand, of Rhetoric and Logic (which is substituted here for Dialectic), and, on the other, of Geometry and Music; and also in that the science corresponding to the Sun (Arithmetic) occupies the rank normally assigned to that star in the astrological order of the planets—the fourth, or midpoint of the septenary—whereas the *Cathars* placed it on the highest rung of their *Mystical Ladder*, as on the corresponding rung on the ladder's opposite upright, Dante places Faith (*Emounah*), that is to say this mysterious *Fede Santa* of which he was himself *Kadosch*.[3]

However, further comment is necessary on this subject, for how is it that correspondences of this kind, which are assimilated to real initiatic degrees, have been attributed to the liberal arts, which, after all, were taught publicly and officially in all the schools? We think they must have been considered in two ways, the one exoteric and the other esoteric. It is possible to superimpose on any profane science another science that is related to the same object but looks at it from a profounder point of view, and which is to that profane science what the higher meanings of the scriptures are to their literal meaning. One could say further that external sciences serve as a mode of expression for higher truths because they are themselves only the symbol of something that is of another order; for as Plato said, the perceptible is only a reflection of the intelligible. The phenomena of nature and the events of history all have a symbolic value in that they express something of the principles upon which they depend, and of which they are the more or less remote consequences. Thus, by means of a suitable transposition, all science and all art can assume a true esoteric value; why then, in the initiations of the Middle Ages, should the expressions drawn from the liberal arts not have played a role comparable to that played in speculative Masonry by language borrowed from the art of the builders? We will go further: to look at things in this way is, after all, to bring

---

3. Concerning the *Mysterious Ladder of the Kadosch* [the Holy Ones], which we shall consider later in this study, see the *Manuel maçonnique* of F∴ Vuilliaume, pl. xvi and pp213–214. We cite the second edition (1830).

them back to their principle; this point of view is, therefore, inherent in their very essence, and not accidentally super-added; and if this is the case, could not the tradition to which it is connected go back to the very origin of the sciences and arts, whereas the exclusively profane viewpoint preponderant in the modern age would only be the result of a general forgetfulness of this tradition? We cannot deal with this question and its many ramifications here, but let us see how Dante himself, in the commentary he gives on his first *Canzone*, points out the way in which he applies to his own work the principles of some of the liberal arts: *O uomini, che vedere non potete la sentenza di questa Canzone, non la rifiutate però; ma ponete mente alla sua bellezza, che è grande, sì per* COSTRUZIONE, *la quale si pertiene alli* GRAMMATICI; *sì per* L'ORDINE DEL SERMONE, *che si pertiene alli* RETTORICI; *si per lo* NUMERO DELLE SUE PARTI, *che si pertiene alli* MUSICI [author's emphasis].[4] Do we not hear an echo of the Pythagorean tradition in this way of relating music and number in a science of rhythm, with all its correspondences; and is it not this same tradition, precisely, that makes possible an understanding of the 'solar' role attributed to arithmetic, which it makes the common center of all the other sciences, and also of the correspondences that unite them, especially of music with geometry, through knowledge of proportion in forms (which finds its direct application in architecture), and, in the case of astronomy, through knowledge of the harmony of the celestial spheres? In what follows we shall see clearly enough what fundamental importance the symbolism of numbers assumes in Dante's work; and even if this symbolism is not uniquely Pythagorean and reappears in other doctrines for the simple reason that truth is one, it is no less permissible to think that from Pythagoras to Virgil, and from Virgil to Dante, the 'chain of the tradition' was undoubtedly unbroken on Italian soil.

4. Here is the translation of this text: 'O men, who cannot see the meaning of this Song, do not however reject it; but pay attention to its beauty, which is great, either for its *construction*, which concerns the *grammarians*; or for the *order of its discourse*, which concerns the *rhetoricians*; or for the *number of its parts*, which concerns the *musicians.*'

3

MASONIC AND HERMETIC PARALLELS

FROM THE GENERAL OBSERVATIONS made thus far we must now return to the following rather remarkable parallels pointed out by Aroux, and to which we alluded above:[1]

Hell represents the *profane world*, *Purgatory* is the place of *initiatic trials*, and *Heaven* is the abode of the *Perfect Ones*, where we find intelligence and love combined and raised to their zenith.... The celestial circle described by Dante[2] begins with the *alti Serafini*, who are the *Principi celesti*, and ends at the lowest ranks of Heaven. Now it happens that certain lower dignitaries of Scottish Masonry (which claims to go back to the Templars, and of which Zerbino, the Scottish prince and Isabelle of Galicia's lover, is the personification in Ariosto's *Orlando Furioso*) are also called princes, *Princes of Mercy*; that their assembly or chapter is called the *Third Heaven*; that they have a *Palladium*,

1. We cite the summary of Aroux's works given by Paul Sédir [1871–1926], *Histoire des Rose-Croix*, pp16–20; second edition, pp13–17 [(Paris: Collection des hérmetistes, 1910); another book by Sédir, with the similar title of *Histoire et doctrines du Rose-Croix*, was published in Bihorel-lez Rouen by A.-L. Legrand, 1932]. The titles of these works by [Eugene] Aroux [1793–1859] are: *Dante hérétique, revolutionnaire et socialiste; revelations d'un catholique sur le moyen age* (Paris: J. Renouard, 1854; also, Paris: Éditions Niclaus, 1939), and *La Comédie de Dante, traduite en vers selon la lettre et commentée selon l'esprit, suivie de la Clef du langage symbolique des Fidèles d'Amour* (Paris: Heritiers J. Renouard, 1856–1857).
2. *Paradiso*, VIII.

or statue of *Truth*, as their symbol, which, like Beatrice, is adorned in the three colors *green*, *white*, and *red*;[3] that their Worshipful Master (whose title is *Most Excellent Prince*), carrying an arrow in his hand and a heart within a triangle on his chest,[4] is a personification of *Love*; and that the mysterious number *nine*, 'by which Beatrice is especially loved'—Beatrice, 'who must be called Love' as Dante says in the *Vita Nuova*—is also assigned to this Worshipful Master, who is surrounded by nine columns and nine torches (each with nine branches and nine lights), and whose age, finally, is eighty-one years, a multiple (or more precisely the square) of nine, Beatrice being said to have died in the eighty-first year of the century.[5]

This *Prince of Mercy*, or *Scottish Trinitarian*, grade, is the 26th of the Scottish Rite. Here is what the F∴ Bouilly says about it in his *Explication des douze écussons* [*the 19th to the 30th*] *qui représentent les emblèmes et les symboles des douze grades philosophiques du Rite Ecossais dit Ancien et Accepté*:

> This grade is, in our opinion, the most inextricable of all those that compose this learned category: it is also given the name *Scottish Trinitarian*.[6] Indeed, everything in this allegory offers the emblem of the Trinity: the background of three colors [green, white, and red]; the representation of *Truth* at the bottom; and, finally, everywhere this indication of the *Great Work of Nature* [to the phases of which the three colors allude], of the constitutive elements of the metals [sulphur, mercury, and salt],[7]

3. It is at least curious that these three colors have in modern times become the national colors of Italy; moreover, a Masonic origin is quite generally attributed to these colors, although it is rather difficult to know whence the idea could have been directly derived.

4. To these distinctive signs we must add a 'crown of golden arrow-heads'.

5. Cf. *Light on Masonry* [David Bernard (Utica: William Williams, 1829)], p250, and *Manuel maçonnique*, pp179–182.

6. We must admit that we do not see the connection that may exist between the complexity of this grade and its name.

7. The alchemical ternary is often likened to that of the constitutive elements of the human being: spirit, soul, and body.

of their fusion and their separation [*solve et coagula*], in a word, of the science of mineral chemistry [or rather of alchemy] which was founded by *Hermes* among the Egyptians, and which gave such power and breadth to medicine [*spagyric*].[8] So true is it that the sciences that lead to happiness and freedom succeed one another and are classified in this admirable order, that it proves the Creator has furnished men with all that can ease their suffering and prolong their sojourn on earth.[9] It is principally in the number *three*, so well represented by the three angles of the *Delta*, which the Christians have made the flamboyant symbol of Divinity, and which goes back to the most remote times,[10] that the skilled observer discovers the primeval source of everything that strikes the mind, enriches the imagination, and gives a just appreciation of social equality.... Therefore, noble Knights, let us not cease to remain *Scottish Trinitarians*, to maintain and honor the number *three* as the emblem of all that constitutes the duties of man, and that at the same time reminds us of the cherished Trinity of our Order, engraved on the columns of our Temples: *Faith, Hope,* and *Charity.*[11]

What we should retain above all from this passage is that the grade concerned, like nearly all those of the same class, presents a clearly

8. The words between brackets have been added to render the text more comprehensible.

9. In these last words we see a discreet allusion to the 'elixir of long life' of the alchemists. The preceding grade (25th), that of the *Knight of the Brazen Serpent*, was explained as 'including a part of the first degree of the *Egyptian Mysteries*, whence *medicine* and the *great art* of compounding remedies originated.'

10. The author no doubt wishes to say 'the symbolic use of which goes back to the most remote times,' for we cannot suppose that he wanted to assign a chronological origin to the number *three* itself.

11. The three colors of this grade are sometimes regarded as symbolizing, respectively, the three theological virtues: white representing Faith, green Hope, and red Charity (or Love). The insignia of this grade of *Prince of Mercy* are a red apron, in the middle of which is painted or embroidered a white and green triangle, and a ribbon of the three colors of the Order worn crosswise, from which is suspended as a jewel an equilateral triangle (or Delta) made of gold. (See *Manuel maçonnique*, p181.)

Hermetic meaning; and what we should particularly note in this regard is the connection of Hermeticism to the Orders of Chivalry.[12] This is not the place to investigate the historical origin of the high grades of Scottish Masonry or to discuss the controversial theory of their descent from the Templars; but, whether there has been a real and direct filiation or only a reconstitution, it is nonetheless certain that most of these grades, and also some found in other rites, seem to be vestiges of organizations that formerly existed independently,[13] and most notably of the ancient Orders of Chivalry, the foundation of which was bound up with the history of the Crusades, that is to say with an epoch when between East and West there existed not only hostile relations, as those who confine themselves to appearances believe, but also active intellectual exchanges, exchanges implemented above all through the mediation of these same Orders. Must we accept that the latter borrowed Hermetic material from the East and then assimilated it, or should we not rather think that from the outset these Orders possessed an esoterism of this kind, and that it was their own initiation that qualified them to enter into relations with the Easterners on this terrain? This again is a question we cannot claim to resolve; but the second hypothesis, though less often entertained than the first,[14] contains nothing implausible for those who recognize, throughout the Middle Ages, the existence of a strictly Western initiatic tradition; and what could further prompt us to accept it is that Orders founded later, which never had dealings with the East, also possessed Hermetic symbolism—for example, the *Golden Fleece*, the very name of

12. A high Mason who seems more versed in the quite modern and profane science called 'history of religions' than in true initiatic knowledge, the Count Goblet d'Alviella, believed he could give a Buddhist interpretation to this purely Hermetic and Christian grade, under the pretext that there is a certain resemblance between the titles *Prince of Mercy* and *Lord of Compassion*.

13. In fact there was an *Order of the Trinitarians* or *Order of Mercy*, which had as aim, at least outwardly, the ransoming of prisoners of war.

14. Some have gone so far as to attribute an exclusively Persian origin to the coat of arms, which has fairly close ties with Hermetic symbolism, whereas in reality the coat of arms has existed from antiquity among many peoples, Western as well as Eastern, and especially among the Celts.

which is the clearest possible allusion to this symbolism. However this may be, in Dante's time Hermeticism certainly existed in the Order of the Temple, as did knowledge of certain doctrines more definitely of Arab origin of which Dante himself seems not to have been ignorant either, and which were no doubt transmitted to him in this way also—a point we shall explain in due course.

Let us return however to the Masonic correspondences mentioned by Aroux, only a few of which we have considered so far. There are several degrees of Scottish Masonry for which Aroux believes he can see a perfect analogy with the nine heavens that Dante traverses with Beatrice. Here are the correspondences that he gives for the seven planetary heavens: to the Moon corresponds the *profane*, to Mercury the *Knight of the Sun* (28th), to Venus the *Prince of Mercy* (26th, green, white, and red), to the Sun the *Great Architect* (12th) or the *Noachite* (21st), to Mars the *Great Scot of the Order of Saint Andrew* or *Patriarch of the Crusades* (29th, red with a white cross), to Jupiter the *Knight of the White and Black Eagle* or *Kadosch* (30th), and to Saturn the *Golden Ladder* of the same *Kadosch*. In truth, some of these attributions seem doubtful to us, especially that of the first heaven as the abode of the profane, for the place of these latter can only be in the 'outer darkness', and in fact have we not already seen that it is hell that represents the profane world, while the different heavens (including that of the Moon) can be reached only after undergoing the initiatic trials of Purgatory? It is well known also that the sphere of the Moon has a special relationship to Limbo; but this is an altogether different aspect of its symbolism and must not be confused with that aspect according to which it is represented as the first heaven. In fact, the Moon is at once *Janua Coeli* and *Janua Inferni*, Diana and Hecate.[15] The ancients knew this very well, as did Dante, who could not have been so mistaken as to accord the profane a celestial abode, even the very lowest.

---

15. These two aspects also correspond to the two solstitial doors; there would be much to say on this symbolism, which the ancient Latins summarized in the figure of Janus. On the other hand, there are some distinctions to make between hell, Limbo, and the 'outer darkness' mentioned in the Gospel; but this would lead us too far afield, and would not affect the present point, which is only concerned in a general way with the separation of the profane world from the initiatic hierarchy.

What is far less debatable is the identification of the symbolic figures seen by Dante: the cross in the heaven of Mars, the eagle in that
of Jupiter, and the ladder in that of Saturn. The cross is assuredly
related to that which, after having been the distinctive sign of the
Orders of Chivalry, still serves as the emblem of several Masonic
grades; and if it is placed in the sphere of Mars, is this not an allusion to the military character of these Orders, their obvious raison
d'être, and to the role they played externally in the military expedi-
tions of the Crusades?[16] As for the other two symbols, it is impossible not to recognize in them those of the *Kadosch Templar*; and at
the same time the eagle, which classical antiquity attributed to Jupiter, as did the Hindus to *Vishnu*,[17] was the emblem of the ancient
Roman Empire (which calls to mind the presence of Trajan[18] in the
eye of that eagle), and it has remained so for the Holy Empire. The
heaven of Jupiter is the abode of the 'wise and just princes' (*Diligite
justitiam, qui judicatis terram*),[19] a correspondence which, like all
those Dante gave to the heavens, is wholly explained in terms of
astrology; and the Hebrew name for the planet Jupiter is *Tsedek*,
meaning 'just'. Of the ladder of the *Kadosch* we have already said
that since the sphere of Saturn is situated immediately above that
of Jupiter, we reach the foot of this ladder by Justice (*Tsedakah*), and
its summit by Faith (*Emunah*). This symbol of the ladder seems to
be of Chaldean origin and to have been brought to the West with
the mysteries of Mithra; at that time it had seven rungs, each fash-
ioned of a different metal according to the correspondence of the

16. One can also note that the heaven of Mars is represented as the abode of the
'martyrs of religion'; there is even a kind of pun on the words *Marte* and *martiri*, of
which one could find other examples elsewhere. Thus the hill of Montmartre was
once the *Mount of Mars* before becoming the *Mount of the Martyrs*. Apropos of this
let us note in passing a rather strange fact: the names of the three martyrs of Montmartre, *Dionysos, Rusticus*, and *Eleutheros*, are all names of Bacchus. Moreover,
Saint Denis, considered the first Bishop of Paris, is commonly identified with Saint
Denys the Areopagite; and in Athens, the Areopagus was also the *Mount of Mars*.

17. The symbolism of the eagle in the different traditions would call for a quite
special study of its own.

18. Trajan, Roman Emperor, AD 98–117. ED.

19. *Paradiso*, XVIII, 91–93. ['Love justice, you who judge the earth.']

metals with the planets, and in biblical symbolism we find Jacob's ladder joining the earth to the heavens, which presents an identical meaning.[20]

'According to Dante, the eighth heaven of Paradise, the starry heaven (or the heaven of the fixed stars), is the *Heaven of the Rose-Cross*. There the *Perfect* are clad in white, and display a symbolism analogous to that of the *Knights of Heredom*;[21] they profess the "evangelical doctrine"—Luther's very own—as opposed to Roman Catholic doctrine.' Here Aroux's interpretation testifies to his frequent confusion of the domains of esoterism and exoterism: true esoterism must lie beyond the oppositions expressed in the outer movements agitating the profane world, and if such movements are sometimes created or invisibly directed by powerful initiatic organizations, one can say that the latter dominate these movements without being part of them, so as to exercise their influence equally upon each of the opposing parties. It is true that the Protestants, and especially the Lutherans, habitually use the word 'evangelical' to describe their own doctrine, and we know also that Luther's seal bore a cross in the center of a rose, and that the Rosicrucian organization, which revealed itself to the public in 1604 (and which Descartes sought vainly to contact), declared itself 'anti-papist'. But it must be said that at the beginning of the seventeenth century the Rosicrucians were already very outward and far removed from the original and genuine Brotherhood of the Rose-Cross, which never constituted a society in the proper sense of the word. As for Luther, he seems to have been only a kind of subordinate agent, no doubt

20. It is not without interest to note further that Saint Peter Damien, with whom Dante converses in the heaven of Saturn, appears in the list (in great part legendary) of the *Imperatores Rosae-Crucis* given in the *Clypeum Veritatis* of Iranaeus Agnostus (1618).

21. The *Order of Heredom of Kilwinning* is the *Great Chapter* of the high grades attached to the *Great Royal Lodge of Edinburgh* and founded, according to tradition, by the king Robert Bruce (Thory, *Acta Latomorum*, vol. 1, p317). The English word *Heredom* (or *heirdom*) means 'heritage' (of the Templars); however, some people derive this name from the Hebrew *Harodim*, a title given to those who directed the workers employed in the construction of the Temple of Solomon. (Cf. our article on this subject in *Études Traditionnelles*, March 1948.)

scarcely conscious of the role he had to play. These various points, moreover, have never been completely elucidated.

Be that as it may, the white robes of the *Elect*, or the *Perfect*, though obviously reminiscent of certain apocalyptic texts,[22] appear above all to allude to the dress of the Templars; and in this respect the following passage is particularly significant:

> Qual è colui che *tace e dicer vuole,*
> Mi trasse Beatrice, e disse: mira
> Quanto è *il convento delle bianche stole!*[23]

Moreover, this interpretation makes it possible to give a very precise meaning to the expression 'the holy militia' found a little further on in lines which seem to express discretely the transformation of Templarism, after its apparent destruction, into Rosicrucianism:[24]

> In forma dunque di *candida rosa*
> Mi si mostrava la *milizia santa,*
> Che nel suo sangue Cristo fece sposa.

To make better understood the symbolism involved in Aroux's last quotation, here is the description of the *Celestial Jerusalem* as it appears in the *Chapter of the Sovereign Princes Rosicrucian*, of the *Order of Heredom of Kilwinning* or the *Royal Order of Scotland*, also named *Knights of the Eagle and the Pelican*:

In the rear [of the last room] there is a picture showing a mountain from which flows a river by whose bank grows a tree bearing

22. Rev. 7:13–14.

23. *Paradiso*, xxx, 127–129. Concerning this passage, we note that the word 'convent' has remained in usage in Masonry to designate its great assemblies.

> *I, yearning to speak and silent*—Beatrice drew me,
> and said: 'Now see how many are in *the convent*
> *of the white robes.* . . .

24. *Paradiso*, xxxi, 1–3. The final verse may refer to the symbolism of the red cross of the Templars.

> Then in the form of a *white rose*, the host
> of the *sacred soldiery* appeared to me,
> all those whom Christ in his own blood espoused.

twelve kinds of fruit. On the summit of the mountain stands a plinth made of twelve precious stones laid in twelve tiers. On top of this plinth is a golden square, and on the face of each side are three angels, each angel bearing the name of one of the twelve tribes of Israel. In this square is a cross, at the center of which lies a lamb. [25]

Here we again find apocalyptic symbolism, and in what follows it will be shown to what extent the cyclical ideas to which it is related are intimately linked to the very plan of Dante's work.

> In cantos xxiv and xxv of the *Paradiso*, we find the triple kiss of the *Rosicrucian Prince*, the pelican, the white tunics (the same as those of the elders in the *Apocalypse*), the sticks of sealing wax, and the three theological virtues of the Masonic Chapters (Faith, Hope, and Charity).[26] The symbolic flower of the Brotherhood of the Rose-Cross (the *Rosa candida* of cantos xxx and xxxi) has been adopted by the Church of Rome as the figure of the Mother of the Savior (*Rosa mystica* of the litanies), and by that of Toulouse (the Albigenses) as the mysterious emblem of the general assembly of the *Fedeli d'Amore*. These metaphors were already employed by the *Paulicians*, predecessors of the *Cathars* in the tenth and eleventh centuries.

We thought it useful to reproduce all these parallels, which are interesting and could no doubt be multiplied without difficulty, but one should not, except perhaps in the cases of the Templars and the original Brotherhood of the Rose-Cross, claim to draw overly firm conclusions with regard to a direct filiation of the different initiatic forms among which we thus ascertain a certain community of symbols. In fact, not only are the fundamentals of the doctrines always

---

25. *Manuel maçonnique*, pp143–144. Cf. Rev. 21.

26. In the Chapters of the Rosicrucians (18th degree Scottish), the names of the three theological virtues are associated, respectively, with the three terms of the motto 'Liberty, Equality, Fraternity'; one could also compare them with what are called 'the three principal pillars of the Temple' in the symbolic grades: 'Wisdom, Strength, Beauty'. To these same three virtues Dante links Saint Peter, Saint James, and Saint John, the three apostles who witnessed the transfiguration.

and everywhere the same, but in addition (which may seem more surprising at first sight) the particular modes of expression themselves often present a striking similarity, even in the case of traditions too remote in time or space to make plausible any immediate influence on each other. To find an effective link in such cases it would no doubt be necessary to go much further back in time than recorded history allows.

Some commentators who have studied the symbolism of Dante's work, such as Rossetti and Aroux, confine themselves to an aspect that we would qualify as external, by which is meant that they have stopped at what could readily be called ritualistic forms, that is, at forms which, for those who are incapable of going further, conceal rather than express their profounder meaning. And as has been very justly said,

> it is natural that it should be thus, for to grasp and understand the allusions and the conventional or allegorical references, one must be acquainted with the object of the allusion or allegory; and in the present case this means an apprehension of the mystical experiences through which true initiation causes the *myste* and the *épopte* to pass. For anyone with some experience of this kind, there can be no doubt about the existence, in the *Divine Comedy* and the *Aeneid*, of a metaphysico-esoteric allegory that simultaneously veils and unveils the successive phases through which the consciousness of the initiate passes in order to attain immortality.[27]

27. Arturo Reghini, art. cit., pp545–546.

4

DANTE AND
ROSICRUCIANISM

THE SAME REPROACH OF INSUFFICIENCY that we have leveled against Rosetti and Aroux can also be addressed to Eliphas Lévi, who, while asserting a relationship to the ancient mysteries, nonetheless saw above all a political or politico-religious application which, in our view, is only of secondary importance, and which is always wrong in supposing that properly initiatic organizations are directly engaged in outer activities. Here, in fact, is what the author says in his *History of Magic*:

> There have been many commentaries and studies on Dante's work, but nobody, as far as we know, has pointed out its true character. The work of the great Ghibelline is a declaration of war on the Papacy through the daring revelation of the mysteries. Dante's epic is Johannite[1] and gnostic; there is a bold application of the diagrams and numbers of the Kabbalah to Christian dogmas, and a secret negation of all that is uncompromising in these dogmas. His journey through the supernatural worlds is accomplished as an initiation into the mysteries of Eleusis and Thebes. It is Virgil who guides and protects him in the circles of the new Tartarus, as though Virgil, the sensitive and melancholic prophet of the destinies of the son of Pollio, were in the eyes of the Florentine poet the illegitimate but real father of the Christian epic.

---

1. Saint John is often considered the head of the *interior* Church, and according to certain conceptions, of which an indication can be found here, some want to oppose him in this respect to Saint Peter, head of the *exterior* Church; the truth is rather that their respective authority does not apply to the same domain.

Thanks to the pagan genius of Virgil, Dante escapes from this abyss on the door of which he had read a sentence of despair; he escapes *by putting his head in place of his feet and his feet in place of his head* (that is to say by taking the opposite view to dogma), and reascends to the light by making use of the devil himself as a monstrous ladder; he escapes the terrible by means of terror, the horrible by means of horror. Hell, it seems, is an impasse only for those who do not know to turn around. Dante rubs the devil the wrong way, if this common expression be permitted, and is set free by his audacity. This is already Protestantism surpassed, and the poet of Rome's enemies has already foreseen Faust rising to Heaven on the head of the vanquished Mephistopheles.[2]

In reality, the wish to 'reveal the mysteries' —supposing such a thing were even possible (which it is not, for there is no real mystery that is not inexpressible)—and the bias of taking 'the view opposite to dogma' or of consciously reversing the meaning and value of symbols, would not be the mark of a very high initiation. Fortunately, we do not see, for our part, any evidence of this in Dante, whose esoterism is on the contrary shrouded by a veil that is rather difficult to penetrate, while at the same time resting on strictly traditional foundations. To make him a precursor of Protestantism, and perhaps of the French Revolution as well, simply because he was an adversary of the papacy in the *political* arena, is to misunderstand his thought entirely or to understand nothing of the spirit of his time.

Something else that seems to us scarcely tenable is the belief that Dante was a 'Kabbalist' in the proper sense of the word. Here we are all the more inclined to be mistrustful, as we know only too well how some of our contemporaries readily delude themselves on this subject, thinking to have found elements of the Kabbalah wherever

---

2. This passage by Eliphas Lévi, like many others (taken mostly from *Dogme et Rituel de la Haute Magie*), was reproduced *verbatim* and with no indication of its provenance by Albert Pike [1809–1891] in his *Morals and Dogma of the Ancient and Accepted Scottish Rite of Freemasonry* [Washington, D.C.: L.H. Jenkins, 1962, and many earlier editions by various publishers], p822, the very title of which moreover is obviously taken from the same source.

there is any kind of esoterism. Have we not seen a Masonic writer solemnly affirm that the *Kabbalah* and *Chivalry* are one and the same thing, and, lacking even the most elementary linguistic notions, that the two words have a common origin?[3] In view of such improbabilities, one will understand the necessity to be wary, and not to be satisfied with vague correspondences in order to make someone into a Kabbalist. Now the Kabbalah is essentially the Hebrew tradition,[4] and we have no proof that a Jewish influence was exerted directly on Dante.[5] What has given rise to such a belief is solely the use he makes of the science of numbers; but even if this science does really exist in the Hebrew Kabbalah, and hold a place therein of the utmost importance, it is nonetheless also found elsewhere.[6] Will it also be claimed under the same pretext that Pythagoras was a Kabbalist?[7] As we have already stated, in this regard it is rather more to Pythagorism than to the Kabbalah that one could link Dante, who quite probably knew from Judaism, above all, what Christianity had preserved from this source in its own doctrine.

'Let us also point out,' Eliphas Lévi goes on to say, 'that Dante's Hell is only a *negative Purgatory.* Let us explain: his Purgatory seems to have formed itself in his Hell as in a mold; it is like the lid or "stopper" as it were of the bottomless pit, and one can understand that in scaling Paradise, the Florentine Titan would like to dispatch

3. Charles Mathieu Limousin, *La Kabbale littérale occidentale: les 32 voies de la sagesse du 'Sefer Ietzirah' expliquées par l'alphabet latin* [Paris: Nouvelle revue, 1897].

4. The word itself means 'tradition' in Hebrew, and unless one writes in this language there is no reason to use it to designate every tradition indiscriminately.

5. One should however say that according to contemporary testimonies Dante had a sustained friendship with the well-educated Jew Immanuel ben Solomon ben Jekuthiel (1270–1330), himself a poet; but it is nonetheless true that we see no trace of specifically Jewish elements in the *Divine Comedy*, whereas Immanuel was himself inspired by the latter in one of his own works, despite the contrary opinion of Israël Zangwill, which the comparison of dates renders quite untenable. [Immanuel ben Solomon, or Immanuel ben Zifroni (also known as Manoello Gindeo or 'Immanuel the Jew'), thought to have lived from 1261 to sometime after 1328. The *Encyclopaedia Judaica* (1972), vol. 8, pp1295–98, confirms Guénon's assertion that Dante influenced this Hebrew poet, and not the other way around. ED.]

6. See *Traditional Forms and Cosmic Cycles*, pt 3, chap. 3. ED.

7. This opinion was put forward by Reuchlin. [Johannes Reuchlin (1455–1522), Christian Kabbalist. ED.]

Purgatory into Hell with a single kick.' This is true in a sense, since
the Mount of Purgatory was formed in the southern hemisphere of
material spewed from the bosom of the earth when the abyss was
dug by Lucifer's fall; yet Hell has nine circles, which are like an
inverted reflection of the nine heavens, while Purgatory has only
seven, the symmetry therefore not being exact in all respects.

'His Heaven is composed of a series of kabbalistic circles divided
by a cross like the pentacle of Ezekiel; at the center of this *cross*
blooms a *rose*, and here we see the symbol of the Rosicrucians
appearing for the first time, publicly revealed and almost categori-
cally explained.' At about the same time, moreover, this very symbol also appeared, though perhaps not so clearly, in another famous
poetic work, *The Romance of the Rose*. Eliphas Lévi thinks that '*The
Romance of the Rose* and the *Divine Comedy* are opposite forms [it
would be more correct to say complementary] of the same work:
the initiation into independence of the spirit, the satirizing of all
contemporary institutions and allegorical formulas of the grand
secrets of the Society of the Rose-Cross,' which in truth did not yet
bear this name and, moreover, we repeat, was never (but for some
more or less deviant branches later) a 'society' constituted with all
the outward forms that this word implies. On the other hand, 'independence of the spirit,' or, to put it better, intellectual independence, was not so exceptional a thing in the Middle Ages as
the moderns usually imagine, and the monks themselves did not
hesitate to express their frank criticisms, evidence of which can be
discerned even in cathedral statuary. In all this there is nothing
properly esoteric; the two works in question contain something far
more profound.

Eliphas Lévi goes on: 'These important manifestations of occultism coincided with the time of the fall of the Templars, since Jean de
Meung or Clopinel, contemporary with Dante's old age, flourished
at the court of Philip the Fair during its finest years. This is a profound book that pretends to be trifling;[8] it is a revelation as learned

8. The same thing can be said of some of Rabelais' works in the sixteenth century, which also have an esoteric import that it would be interesting to study more
closely.

as that of Apuleius on the mysteries of occultism. The rose of
Flamel, that of Jean de Meung, and that of Dante, were born of the
same bush.'[9]

On these lines we would only caution that the word 'occultism',
invented by Eliphas Lévi himself, is hardly suitable to designate
what pre-dated him, especially when one reflects on what contemporary occultism has become, which, in claiming to be a restoration
of esoterism, has succeeded only in becoming a crude counterfeit of
it because its leaders have never been in possession of true principles or of any genuine initiation. Eliphas Lévi would no doubt be
the first to disavow his would-be successors, to whom he was certainly very much superior intellectually while at the same time he
was nonetheless far from being as profound as he wished to appear,
wrongly viewing everything through the mentality of an 1848 revolutionary. If we have spent some time discussing his opinions, it is
because we know how great his influence has been, even upon those
who scarcely understood him, and because we think it best to fix the
limits within which his competence can be acknowledged; his principal shortcoming, which was that of his time, was to put social pre-
occupations in the foreground and to mix them indiscriminately
with everything. In Dante's day one certainly knew better how to
assign to each thing its proper place in the universal hierarchy.

What is of particular interest in this for the history of esoteric
doctrines is the finding that several important manifestations of
these doctrines coincided, within just a few years, with the destruction of the Order of the Temple. There is an unquestionable connection between these events, although it is rather difficult to deter-
mine it precisely. In the early years of the fourteenth century, and
doubtless already in the course of the preceding century, there was
thus, in France as well as in Italy, a secret tradition ('occult' if one
likes, but not 'occultist'), the very one that later was to bear the

---

9. Eliphas Lévi, *Histoire de la Magie*, 1860, pp359–360. It is worth noting apropos of this that there exists an Italian adaptation of the *Romance of the Rose*, entitled
Il Fiore, whose author, 'Ser Durante Fiorentino', appears to be none other than
Dante himself, whose real name was, in fact, Durante, of which Dante is only an
abbreviated form.

name of Rosicrucianism. The denomination *Fraternitas Rosae-Cru-cis* appears for the first time in 1374, or, according to some (notably Michael Maier),[10] in 1413; and the legend of *Christian Rosenkreuz*, the supposed founder whose name and life are purely symbolic, was perhaps fully formed only in the sixteenth century; but we have just seen that the Rose-Cross symbol is certainly much earlier.

This esoteric doctrine, whatever particular designation one may wish to give it—if it is necessary to do so at all—prior to its appearance as Rosicrucianism in the strict sense of the word, presented some characteristics that allow us to join it with what is generally called Hermeticism. The history of the Hermetic tradition is intimately linked to that of the Orders of Chivalry, and was preserved at the time in question by initiatic organizations such as the *Fede Santa* and the *Fedeli d'Amore*, as also by the *Massenie of the Holy Grail*. Of the latter the historian Henri Martin says,[11] specifically apropos of the romances of chivalry, which remain to this day among the great literary manifestations of esoterism in the Middle Ages:

> In the *Titurel*, the legend of the *Grail* reached its final and splendid transfiguration under the influence of ideas that Wolfram[12] appears to have taken from France, and particularly from the Templars in the south of France. It was no longer in the British Isles but in Gaul, on the border of Spain, that the *Grail* was kept. A hero named Titurel founded a temple in order to deposit the holy *Vessel* there, and it was the prophet Merlin, initiated by Joseph of Arimathea in person to the plan of the Temple par excellence, the Temple of Solomon, who directed this mysterious construction.[13] The *Knighthood of the Grail* here becomes the *Massenie*, that is to say an ascetic Freemasonry,

10. Michael Maier (1568–1622), German alchemist and Rosicrucian. ED.
11. *Histoire de France*, vol. III, pp 398–399.
12. The Swabian Templar Wolfram von Eschenbach, author of *Parsival* [*Perceval*] and imitator of the Benedictine satirist Guyot de Provins, whom he designates under the singularly deformed name of 'Kyot de Provence'.
13. Henri Martin adds this note: 'Perceval ends up by transferring the Grail to India and rebuilding the Temple there; and it is *Prester John*, that fantastic chief of an imaginary oriental Christianity, who inherits the guardianship of the holy *Vessel*.'

whose members called themselves the *Templists*; and we can grasp here the intention of linking up to a common center, represented by this ideal Temple, the *Order of the Templars* and the numerous *fraternities of builders* which at that time were renewing the architecture of the Middle Ages. We catch here a glimpse of many openings on to what could be called the subterranean history of those times, which are far more complex than is generally believed.... What is rather curious, and can hardly be doubted, is that modern Freemasonry goes back step by step to the *Massenie of the Holy Grail*.[14]

It would perhaps be imprudent to adopt too exclusively the opinion just expressed, because the ties of modern Masonry with earlier organizations are themselves also extremely complex; nonetheless it is useful to take them into account, for here one can see at least an indication of one of the actual origins of Masonry. All this can help us grasp, at least to a certain extent, the means by which esoteric doctrines were transmitted throughout the Middle Ages, as well as the obscure filiation of initiatic organizations during this same period, when they were truly secret in the most complete sense of the word.

14. We touch here on a very important point, but one which we cannot treat without wandering too far from our subject: there is a very close relationship between the symbolism of the *Grail* and that of the 'common center' to which Henri Martin alludes, although he appears not to suspect the profound reality involved, any more than he understands what is symbolized, in the same order of ideas, by the name of *Prester John* and his mysterious kingdom.

5

EXTRA-TERRESTRIAL JOURNEYS IN DIFFERENT TRADITIONS

ONE question that seems to have greatly preoccupied most of Dante's commentators is that of what sources to acknowledge for his conception of the descent into Hell; and this is also one of the points that most clearly highlights the incompetence of those who have only studied these questions in a completely 'profane' manner. In fact, this matter can only be understood through a certain acquaintance with the stages of initiation, and it is this that we shall now try to explain.

If Dante takes Virgil for his guide in the first two parts of his journey, the principal reason, as everyone recognizes, is doubtless his recollection of the sixth canto of the *Aeneid*, but we must add that this is because Virgil's work is no mere poetic fiction, but, on the contrary, gives incontestable proof of initiatic knowledge. It is not without reason that the practice of the *sortes virgilianae* [casting of lots] was so widespread in the Middle Ages; and if people have wanted to make a magician of Virgil, this is only a popular and exoteric distortion of a profound truth which those who likened his work to Holy Writ—even if they did so only for a divinatory usage of very relative interest—probably sensed better than they could express.

On the other hand, it is not difficult to see in this connection that Virgil himself had some predecessors among the Greeks, and apropos of this to recall the voyage of Ulysses to the country of the Cimmerians and the descent of Orpheus into the Underworld; but does the concordance we have noticed in all of this prove nothing more than a series of borrowings or successive imitations? The truth is that what is involved here has a close connection to the mysteries of antiquity, and that the various poetic and legendary accounts are only translations of one and the same reality: the golden bough [*rameau d'or*] that Aeneas, guided by the Sibyl, first goes to gather in the forest (that very *selva selvaggia* where Dante also sets the beginning of his poem), is the same bough that was carried by the Eleusinian initiates, reminding one further of the acacia of modern Masonry, 'token of resurrection and immortality'. What is more, Christianity presents us with a similar symbolism: in the Catholic liturgy it is Palm Sunday [*la fête des Rameaux*][1] that opens Holy Week, which encompasses the death of Christ, his descent into Hell, and his resurrection, to be followed shortly thereafter by his glorious ascension; and it is precisely on Holy Monday that Dante's recital commences, as if to indicate that it is in undertaking the quest of the mysterious bough that he loses his way in the dark forest where he will meet Virgil; and his journey across the worlds will last until Easter Sunday, that is to say until the Day of Resurrection.

On the one hand, death and descent into the hells; on the other, resurrection and ascension to the heavens. These are two inverse and complementary phases, of which the first is the necessary preparation for the second, and can easily be recognized in the description of the Hermetic 'Great Work'; the same is clearly affirmed in all traditional doctrines. In Islam, for example, we encounter the episode of Muhammad's 'nocturnal journey', consisting of the same descent into the infernal regions (*isrā*), followed by ascension to the various paradises or celestial spheres (*mir'āj*). There is a striking similarity between certain accounts of this 'nocturnal journey' and Dante's poem, so much so that some have seen in them one of the principal sources of Dante's inspiration. Don Miguel Asìn Palacios has shown the multiple relationships that exist in respect not only

---

1. The Latin name for this festival is *Dominica in Palmis* [Palm Sunday]. The palm and the bough are obviously one and the same thing; and the palm, taken as an emblem for the martyrs, also has the meaning we are indicating here. Recall also the popular name *Pâques fleuries* [for Palm Sunday, literally 'flowery Pascha'], which very clearly expresses, although those who use it today are ignorant of it, the relationship of the symbolism of this festival to the resurrection.

of content but also of form, between the *Divine Comedy* (not to speak of some passages from the *Vita Nuova* and the *Convivio*) on the one hand, and both the *Kitāb al-Isrā* (The Book of the Nocturnal Journey) and the *Futūḥāt al-Makkiyah* (The Meccan Revelations) of Muḥyi'd-Dīn ibn al-'Arabi on the other, works that were written about eighty years before Dante's. He concludes that these analogies, taken alone, are more numerous than all of those that other commentators have succeeded in establishing between Dante's work and the literatures of all other countries.[2] Here are some examples:

> In an adaptation of the Islamic legend, a wolf and a lion bar the pilgrim's route; similarly, the panther, the lion, and the she-wolf force Dante to draw back.... Heaven sends Virgil to Dante and Gabriel to Muhammad, each satisfying the pilgrim's curiosity during the journey. Hell is heralded in the two legends by identical signs: violent and confused tumult, blasts of fire.... The architecture of Dante's Inferno is modeled on the Muslim Hell: both consist of an immense funnel formed by a series of levels, with circular steps or stairs descending gradually to the bottom of the earth; each of them harbors a category of sinners whose culpability and punishment grow worse the deeper the circle in which they dwell. Each level is subdivided into several others, allotted to various categories of sinners; finally, both of these Hells are located under the city of Jerusalem.... On leaving Hell, in order to purify himself and ascend to Paradise, Dante undergoes a triple ablution. In the Islamic tradition, a similar triple ablution purifies souls: before entering Heaven, they are plunged successively into the waters of the three rivers that fertilize the Garden of Abraham.... The architecture of the celestial spheres across which the Ascension occurs is identical in the two legends: the souls of the blessed are ranged in the nine heavens

---

2. Miguel Asìn Palacios, *La Escatologia Musulmana en la Divina Comedia: sequida de la historia y critica de una polemica* (Madrid: Editorial Maestre, 1961). [See *Islam and the Divine Comedy*, tr. Harold Sutherland (London: Frank Cass & Co., 1968).] Cf. Edgar Blochet, *Les Sources orientales de 'la divine Comédie'* (Paris: J. Maisonneuve, 1901).

according to their respective merits, and are gathered finally in the Empyrean or last sphere. . . . Just as Beatrice stands aside that Saint Bernard may guide Dante during the final stages, so does Gabriel abandon Muhammad near the throne of God, to which he will be drawn by a luminous garland. . . . The final apotheosis of both ascensions is the same: the two travelers, raised to the presence of God, describe Him as a center of intense light surrounded by nine concentric circles formed by close files of innumerable angelic spirits who emit luminous rays; one of the circular ranks nearest to the center is that of the Cherubim; each circle encloses the circle immediately below it, and all nine turn unceasingly around the divine center. . . . The infernal stages, the astronomical heavens, the circles of the mystic rose, the angelic choirs that surround the center of divine light, the three circles symbolizing the trinity of persons: all are borrowed word for word by the Florentine poet from Muḥyi 'd-Dīn ibn al-'Arabī.[3]

Such coincidences, extending to the most precise details, cannot be accidental, and we have many reasons to think that to a considerable extent Dante indeed was inspired by the writings of Muḥyi 'd-Dīn. But how could he have known these writings? One possible intermediary is Brunetto Latini, who had lived in Spain, but this hypothesis hardly seems satisfactory because, though he was born in Murcia (hence his nickname *Al-Andalusi*), Muḥyi 'd-Dīn did not spend all his life in Spain, dying in fact in Damascus; and though his disciples were spread throughout the Islamic world—primarily in Syria and Egypt—it is unlikely that his works entered the public domain at that time; indeed, some have never yet been published. Muḥyi 'd-Dīn was in fact anything but the 'mystical poet' that Palacios imagines him to be. What must be acknowledged here is that in Islamic esoterism Muḥyi 'd-Dīn is referred to as *al-Shaykh al-Akbar*, that is, the greatest of spiritual Masters, the Master par excellence; that his doctrine is purely metaphysical; and that several of the principal initiatic Orders in Islam, among them the highest and

3. A. Cabaton, 'La Divine Comédie et l'Islam', in *Revue de l'Histoire des Religions*, 1920; this article contains a résumé of the work of Miguel Asìn Palacios.

least accessible, proceed from him directly. We have already indicated that in the thirteenth century, that is to say in Muḥyi 'd-Dīn's own era, such organizations were in contact with the Orders of Chivalry, which for us explains the transmission noted. Were it otherwise, and had Dante known of Muḥyi 'd-Dīn through 'profane' channels, why did he never name him, as he did two exoteric philosophers of Islam, Avicenna and Averroës?[4] Furthermore, it is recognized that there were some Islamic influences at the beginnings of Rosicrucianism; it is to this that the supposed journeys of Christian Rosenkreuz to the East allude. But the real origin of Rosicrucianism, as we have already stated, lies precisely in the Orders of Chivalry; and it was these that formed the true intellectual link between the East and the West in the Middle Ages.

Modern Western critics, who regard Muhammad's 'nocturnal journey' as nothing more than a poetic legend, claim that this legend is not specifically Islamic, or Arab, but of Persian origin, for an account of a similar journey exists in a Mazdean book, the *Ardā Vīrāf Nāmeh*.[5] Some think it necessary to go back much further, to India, where in Brahmanism as well as in Buddhism we indeed meet a multitude of symbolic descriptions of the diverse states of existence under the form of a hierarchically organized ensemble of heavens and hells; and some even go so far as to suppose that Dante may have been directly influenced by doctrines from India.[6] For those who see all this as mere 'literature', such a way of looking at things is understandable, although it is rather difficult, even from the historical point of view, to admit that Dante could have known anything of India other than through the intermediary of the Arabs. For us,

4. *Inferno*, IV, 143–144.

5. Blochet, 'Études sur l'Histoire religieuse de l'Islam', in *Revue de l'Histoire des Religions*, 1899. A French translation of *Livre d'Ardā Vīrāf*, by M.A. Barthélemy, was published in 1887.

6. Angelo de Gubernatis, 'Dante e l'India', in *Giornale della Società asiatica italiana*, vol. III, 1889, pp 3–19; 'Le Type indien de Lucifer chez Dante', in *Actes du Xe Congrès des Orientalistes*. Cabaton, in the article cited above, points out that 'Ozanam had already glimpsed a double Islamic and Indian influence on Dante' ('Essai sur la philosophie de Dante', pp 198 ff); but we must say that the work of Ozanam, in spite of the reputation it enjoys, seems to us extremely superficial.

however, these similarities demonstrate nothing else than the unity of doctrine in all traditions. There is nothing astonishing in finding everywhere expressions of the same truths, but precisely in order not to be astonished one must first of all know that these are truths, and not more or less arbitrary fictions. Where there are only resemblances of a general order there is no reason to conclude that there must have been direct communication, for such a conclusion would be justified only if the same ideas were expressed in an identical form, such as is the case with Muḥyi 'd-Dīn and Dante. It is certain that what we find in Dante is in perfect accord with the Hindu theories of the worlds and cosmic cycles, though it is not clothed in a properly Hindu form; and this accord necessarily exists among all who are conscious of the same truths, however they may have acquired knowledge of them.

6

THE THREE WORLDS

THE DIFFERENTIATION OF THE THREE WORLDS, which constitutes the general plan of the *Divine Comedy*, is common to all traditional doctrines; but it takes diverse forms, and even in India there are two versions that, neither coinciding nor standing in contradiction, correspond simply to different points of view. According to one version the three worlds are the Hells, the Earth, and the Heavens; according to the other, where the Underworld is no longer envisaged, they are the Earth, the Atmosphere (or intermediary region), and Heaven. In the first, one must admit that the intermediary region is considered a simple prolongation of the terrestrial world, in much the same way that Dante views Purgatory, which can be identified with this same region. On the other hand, and taking this assimilation into account, the second division is strictly equivalent to the distinctions made in Catholic doctrine between the Church Militant, the Church Suffering, and the Church Triumphant. Here again there can be no question of Hell. Finally, a variable number of subdivisions is frequently envisaged for the Heavens and Hells, but in all such cases it is a question of a hierarchical apportionment of the levels of existence, which are really of an indefinite multiplicity and can be classified differently according to the analogical correspondences that one selects as a basis for symbolic representation.

The heavens are the superior states of the being; the hells, as the name itself indicates, are the inferior states. When we say 'superior' and 'inferior' this must be understood in relation to the human or terrestrial state, which is naturally taken as a term of comparison because it serves necessarily as our point of departure. It is easy to understand that true initiation, by which we mean the conscious acquisition of superior states, can be described symbolically as an ascension or 'celestial journey'; but one could ask why this ascension must be preceded by a descent into Hell. There are several reasons for this, but these we could not fully explain now without entering into long digressions that would lead us too far from the special subject of our present study. We will say only that this descent is on the one hand a sort of recapitulation of the states that logically precede the human state and that have determined its particular conditions, and that must also partake in the 'transformation' that is to be accomplished; on the other hand, the descent allows the manifestation according to certain modalities of the possibilities of an inferior order that the being still carries in an undeveloped state, and that must be exhausted before it is possible to attain the realization of the superior states. It must be emphasized moreover that there can be no question of the being actually returning to those states through which it has already passed; it can only explore these states indirectly, by becoming aware of the traces they have left in the most obscure regions of the human state itself; and this is why Hell is represented symbolically as situated in the interior of the Earth.

The heavens, on the contrary, are the superior states, and not merely their reflection in the human state, of which the uppermost prolongations constitute only the intermediary region, or Purgatory, the mountain on whose summit Dante places the Terrestrial Paradise. The real aim of initiation is not merely the restoration of the 'Edenic state', which is only a stage on a path that must lead much higher since it is beyond this stage that the 'celestial journey' really begins, but rather the *active* conquest of the 'supra-human' states; for as Dante remarks, following the Gospel, 'Regnum coelorum *violenzia pate*,'[1] and this is one of the essential differences that exists between initiates and mystics. In other words, the human state must first be brought to its full development by the integral realization of its own possibilities (and this is what must be understood here by the 'Edenic state'); however, far from being the end, this will be only the foundation on which the being will have to stand in order to *salire alle stelle*,[2] that is to say to raise itself to the

---

1. *Paradiso*, xx, 94 [The Kingdom of Heaven *suffers itself to move*].
2. *Purgatorio*, xxxiii, 145. [Leap to the stars.] It is remarkable that the three parts of the poem all end with the same word *stelle*, as if to affirm the very particular importance that astrological symbolism had for Dante. The *Inferno's* last words,

superior states, symbolized by the planetary and stellar spheres in the language of astrology, and by the angelic hierarchies in that of theology. There are therefore two stages to distinguish in the ascension, but the first is in truth only an ascension in relation to ordinary humanity. The height of a mountain, whatever it may be, is nothing in comparison to the distance that separates the Earth from the heavens; in reality therefore it is more an extension since it is the complete unfolding of the human state. The unfolding of the possibilities of the total being is thus effected first in the sense of 'amplitude', and then in that of 'exaltation', to use terms borrowed from Islamic esoterism; and we will add that this distinction of two stages corresponds to the ancient division of the 'lesser mysteries' and the 'greater mysteries'.

The three phases to which the three parts of the *Divine Comedy* respectively relate can be further explained by the Hindu doctrine of the three *gunas*, which are the qualities, or rather the fundamental tendencies, from which all manifested being proceeds. Beings are distributed hierarchically in the totality of the three worlds, that is, in all the degrees of universal existence, according to which tendency predominates in them. The three *gunas* are: *sattva*, or conformity to the pure essence of Being, which is identical to the light of Knowledge and is symbolized by the luminosity of the celestial spheres that represent the superior states; *rajas*, or impulsion, which provokes the expansion of the being in a given state (such as the human), or, if one wishes, the unfolding of this being up to a certain level of existence; and finally *tamas*, or obscurity, which is identified with ignorance, the dark root of the being considered in its inferior states. Thus *sattva*, which is an upward tendency, refers to

---

riveder le stelle [look once more upon the stars], characterize the return to the properly human state, from which it is possible to perceive a sort of reflection of the superior states; the last words of the *Purgatorio* are precisely those we are explaining here. As for the *Paradiso*'s final verse, *L'Amor chi muove il Sole e l'altre stelle* [The Love which moves the sun and the other stars], it designates, as the final goal of the 'celestial journey', the divine center that lies beyond all the spheres, and that is, according to Aristotle's expression, the 'unmoved mover' of all things; the name 'Love' [*Amour*], which is attributed to it, could give rise to some interesting considerations in relation to the symbolism proper to initiation in the Orders of Chivalry.

the superior and luminous states, or to the heavens, and *tamas*, which is a downward tendency, to the inferior and dark states, or to the Hells. *Rajas*, which could be represented as an extension in the horizontal sense, refers to the intermediary world, which is here the 'world of man' since it is our level of existence that we are taking as term of comparison, and which we must regard as consisting of the Earth together with Purgatory, that is, of the whole of the corporeal and the psychic world. We see that this corresponds exactly to the first of the two ways of envisaging the division of the three worlds that we mentioned previously; and the passage from one to another of these three worlds can be described as resulting from a change in the general direction of the being, or from a change in the *guna* that determines this direction by virtue of its predominance. There is a Vedic text in which the three *gunas* are presented in precisely this way, the one changing into the other in an ascending order: 'All was *tamas*: It [the Supreme *Brahma*] decreed a change, and *tamas* took the complexion [that is to say the nature] of *rajas* [intermediate between darkness and luminosity]; and *rajas*, having been commanded once more, assumed the nature of *sattva*.' This text gives a sort of schema of the organization of the three worlds, starting from the primordial chaos of possibilities, and conforming to the order of generation and the sequence of the cycles of universal existence. Moreover, in order to realize all its possibilities, each being must pass, in the particular way suited to its nature, through states that correspond, respectively, to these different cycles; and this is why initiation, which aims at the total realization of the being, must be effected through these same phases: the initiatic process rigorously reproduces the cosmogonic process, according to the constitutive analogy of the macrocosm and microcosm.[3]

3. The theory of the three *gunas*, relating to all the possible modes of universal manifestation, is naturally susceptible of multiple applications. One of these applications, which especially concerns the world of the senses, is found in the cosmological theory of the elements; but here we have had to consider only its most general significance, since it was only a question of explaining the distribution of the whole of manifestation according to the hierarchical division of the three worlds, and of indicating the importance of this distribution from the initiatic point of view. [The text is from the *Maitrayana Upanishad*, v. 2. ED.]

7

THE SYMBOLIC
NUMBERS

BEFORE PASSING ON to some considerations relating to the doctrine of cosmic cycles, we must first make a few remarks concerning the role that the symbolism of numbers plays in Dante's work. On this subject we have found some very interesting information in a work by Rodolfo Benini,[1] who, however, has not drawn all the conclusions these appear to imply. It is true that this work is a study of the original plan of the *Inferno*, and thus primarily a literary undertaking, but the findings to which it can in fact lead have a much more considerable import.

According to Benini, there were for Dante three pairs of numbers having a symbolic significance par excellence: 3 and 9, 7 and 22, 515 and 666. For the first two numbers there is no difficulty whatsoever: everyone knows that the general division of the poem is ternary, and we have just explained the profound reasons for this; on the other hand, we have already recalled that 9 is the number of Beatrice, as seen in the *Vita Nuova*. Moreover, this number 9 is directly linked to 3, of which it is the square, and could be called a triple ternary. It is also the number of the angelic hierarchies, and therefore that of the heavens as well as of the infernal circles, for there is a certain relation of inverse symmetry between the heavens and the hells. As for the number 7, which we find especially in the divisions of Purgatory, all traditions are agreed in regarding it as a sacred number, and we do not believe it useful to enumerate here the many applications to

---

1. 'Per la restituzione della Cantica dell'Inferno alla sua forma primitiva', in *Nuovo Patto*, September/November 1921, pp 506–532.

which it gives rise. We will only recall, as one of the principal ones, the idea of the seven planets, which serves as the basis for a multitude of analogical correspondences (an example of which we have seen in reference to the seven liberal arts). The number 22 is linked to 7 through the ratio $^{22}/_{7}$, which is the approximation of the ratio of the circumference to the diameter of a circle, so that the combination of these two numbers represents the circle, which is the most perfect form for Dante as for the Pythagoreans (and all the divisions of each of the three worlds have this circular form). Moreover, 22 combines the symbols of two of the 'elementary movements' of Aristotelian physics: *locomotion*, represented by two, and *alteration*, represented by 20, as Dante himself explains in the *Convivio*.[2] Such, in any case, are the interpretations given by Benini for this last number. For our part, although acknowledging them to be perfectly correct, we must say that this number does not seem to us so fundamental as he thinks, being derived in all likelihood from another number which the same author regards as of only secondary importance, whereas in reality its significance is much greater: the number 11, of which 22 is only a multiple.

We must in fact insist on this point somewhat, and say at the outset that this omission on Benini's part surprised us all the more as his entire work rests upon the fact that in the *Inferno* most of the complete scenes or episodes into which the various cantos are divided comprise exactly eleven, or twenty-two, stanzas (some have only ten). There are also a number of preludes and finales of seven stanzas; and if these proportions have not always been preserved intact, it is because the original plan of the *Inferno* has been subsequently modified. Under these circumstances, why should 11 not be at least as important as 22? These two numbers can be found associated again in the dimensions assigned to the lowest circles of the 'pit of Hell', the circumferences of which are 11 and 22 miles respectively. But 22 is not the only multiple of 11 that occurs in the poem. There is also 33, the number of cantos into which each of the three parts is

2. The third 'elementary movement', that of *growth*, is represented by 1,000; and the sum of the three symbolic numbers is 1,022, which, according to Dante, the 'sages of Egypt' regarded as the number of the fixed stars.

divided. Only the *Inferno* has 34, but the first canto is more by way of a general introduction that completes the total number 100 for the work as a whole. On the other hand, when we know how important rhythm was for Dante, we can imagine that his choice of a line of 11 syllables was not an arbitrary one, any more than was the stanza of three lines, which recalls for us the ternary: each stanza has 33 syllables, in the same way as the sets of 11 and 22 stanzas just mentioned contain 33 and 66 lines respectively; and the various multiples of 11 that we find here all have a particular symbolic value. It is quite insufficient therefore to limit oneself, as does Benini, to introducing 10 and 11 between 7 and 22 in order to construct a 'tetrachord that has a vague resemblance to the Greek tetrachord,' the explanation of which seems to us rather awkward.

The truth is that the number 11 has played a considerable role in the symbolism of certain initiatic organizations; and as for its multiples, we will simply recall this: 22 is the number of letters in the Hebrew alphabet, and we know of their importance in the Kabbalah; 33 is the number of years of Christ's terrestrial life, found again in the symbolic age of Masonic Rosicrucianism and the number of degrees of Scottish Masonry; 66, in Arabic, is the total numeric value of the name of Allah, while 99 is the number of the principal divine attributes according to Islamic tradition; and many other correspondences could no doubt be found. Apart from the diverse meanings that can be assigned to 11 and to its multiples, their use by Dante constitutes a veritable 'sign of recognition' in the strictest sense of this expression; and this is precisely where we find the real reason for the modifications the *Inferno* had to undergo after its first draft. Among the reasons for these modifications, Benini envisages some changes in the chronological and architectonic plan of the work that are doubtless possible, but for which there does not appear to be any clear proof; but he also mentions 'the *new facts* that the poet wanted to take into account in the system of prophecies,' and it is here that he seems to approach the truth, especially when he adds: 'for example, the death of Pope Clement V, which occurred in 1314, just when the first draft of the *Inferno* must have been completed.' In fact the true reason, in our eyes, is the series of events that took place from 1300 to 1314, namely

the destruction of the Order of the Temple, and its various conse- ∨
quences.[3] Dante, moreover, was unable to refrain from pointing to
these events when, in making Hugues Capet foretell the crimes of
Philip the Fair, after having spoken of the outrage that the latter
inflicted 'upon Christ through his Vicar', he continues:

> Veggio il nuovo Pilato si crudele
> Che ciò nol sazia, ma, senza decreto,
> Porta nel *tempio* le cupide vele.[4]

What is more astonishing, the following stanza[5] contains, in specific
terms, the *Nekam Adonaï*[6] of the *Kadosch Templars*:

> O *Signor mio*, quando sarò io lieto
> A veder la *vendetta*, che, nascosa,
> Fa dolce l'ira tua nel tuo segreto?

---

3. It is interesting to consider the sequence of these dates: in 1307 Philip the Fair,
in agreement with [Pope] Clement V, has the Grand Master and the principal dignitaries of the Order of the Temple imprisoned (to the number of 72 it is said, again
a symbolic number); in 1308 Henri of Luxembourg is elected emperor; in 1312 the
Order of the Temple is officially abolished; in 1313 the Emperor Henri VII dies mys-
teriously, no doubt poisoned; in 1314 the final destruction of the Templars, whose
trial had lasted seven years, takes place; and the same year King Philip the Fair and
Pope Clement V die in their turn.

4. *Purgatorio*, xx, 90–93.

> I see another Pilate, so full of spite
> not even that suffices: his swollen sails
> enter the very *Temple* without right.

For Dante, the driving force of Philip the Fair is avarice and cupidity; there was
perhaps a closer relationship than is supposed between two actions imputable to
this king: the destruction of the Order of the Temple and the debasement of the
coinage.

5. *Purgatorio*, xx, 94–96.

> O *God, my Lord*, when shall my soul rejoice
> to see Thy *retribution*, which, lying hidden,
> sweetens Thine anger in Thy secret choice?

6. In Hebrew, these words mean: 'Vengeance O Lord!' *Adonai* should be translated more literally as 'my Lord', and it will be noted that this is exactly how it is
rendered in Dante's text.

These are most certainly the 'new facts' that Dante had to take into account, and this for other motives than those that could occur to one who ignores the nature of the organizations to which he belonged. These organizations, which proceeded from the Order of the Temple and were to inherit a part of its legacy, had to conceal themselves with far greater care than before, especially after the death of their outward leader, Emperor Henry VII of Luxembourg, whose seat in the highest part of the heavens[7] Beatrice had shown to Dante by way of anticipation. From then on, it was advisable to conceal the 'sign of recognition' to which we have referred: the divisions of the poem where the number eleven appeared most clearly had to be, not suppressed, but rendered less visible, in such a way as to be recognizable only by those who were acquainted with their raison d'être and meaning. And if we reflect that six centuries went by before their existence was revealed publicly, it must be admitted that the intended precautions were well devised, and not lacking in effectiveness.[8]

On the other hand, at the same time that he was making these changes to the first part of his poem, Dante was taking the opportunity to insert into it some new references to other symbolic numbers; and here is what Benini says: 'Dante then thought of adjusting the intervals between the prophecies and other salient features of the poem in such a way that they would correspond to

7. *Paradiso*, xxx, 124–148. This passage concerns precisely the *convento delle bianche stole* [gathering of white robes]. The organizations in question had taken *Altri* as a password, which Aroux (*Dante hérétique, révolutionnaire et socialiste*, p227) interprets as: *Arrigo Lucemburghese Teutonico, Romano Imperatore*; we think that the word *Teutonico* is incorrect and should be replaced by *Templar*. It is true however that there must have been a certain connection between the Order of the Temple and that of the *Teutonic Knights*; it is not without reason that they were founded almost simultaneously, the first in 1118 and the second in 1128. Aroux supposes that the word *altri* could be interpreted as has just been mentioned in a certain passage of Dante (*Inferno* ix, 9), and that, in the same way, the word *tal* (idem, viii 130, and ix, 8) could be translated as *Teutonico Arrigo Lucemburghese*.

8. The number 11 has been kept in the ritual of the 33rd Scottish degree, where it is associated precisely with the date of the abolition of the Order of the Temple, calculated according to the Masonic era, not the common calendar.

one another according to some determined numbers of lines, quite naturally chosen from among the symbolic numbers. In short, Dante substituted for the earlier plan a system of consonances and rhythmic periods far more complicated and *secret*, as befits a revelatory language spoken by those who see the future. Here the famous numbers 515 and 666 make their appearance, numbers that recur frequently in the trilogy: 666 lines separate Ciacco's prophecy from that of Virgil, and 515 Farinata's prophecy from that of Ciacco; 666 lines are interposed again between the prophecy of Brunetto Latini and that of Farinata, and again 515 between the prophecy of Nicolas III and that of Master Brunetto.' These numbers 515 and 666, which we see alternate so regularly, are opposed to each other in the symbolism adopted by Dante: we know in fact that 666 is the 'number of the beast' in the Apocalypse, and that innumerable, and often fanciful, calculations have been indulged in to find the name of the Antichrist, of whom it must represent the numeric value, 'for this number is a number of man.'[9] On the other hand, 515 is expressly invested with a meaning directly contrary to 666 in Beatrices's prediction: '*A cinquecento diece e cinque*, messo di Dio....' [Guénon's emphasis].[10] Some have thought this 515 equivalent to the mysterious *Veltro*, enemy of the she-wolf, which is also identified with the apocalyptic beast;[11] and it has even been suggested that both symbols designated Henry of Luxembourg.[12] We do not intend to discuss the significance of the *Veltro*[13] here, but neither do we believe it necessary to see in it an allusion to a particular person; for us, it concerns only one of the aspects of the general conception that

9. Rev. 13:18.

10. *Purgatorio*, xxxiii, 43–44. ['...by God's decree, *five hundred, ten and five....*']

11. *Inferno* 1, 100–111. We know that the she-wolf was the first symbol of Rome, but that it was replaced by the eagle during the imperial epoch.

12. Ernesto Giacomo Parodi [1862–1923], *Poesia e Storia nella Divina Commedia* [Vicenza: Neri Pazza Editore, 1965].

13. The *Veltro* is a greyhound, a dog, and Aroux suggests the possibility of a sort of play on words between *cane* [Italian for 'dog'] and the title of *Khan* borne by the Tartar chiefs; thus a name like *Can Grande della Scala*, Dante's protector, could well have had a double sense. This parallel is not unlikely, for it is not the only example

Dante had of the empire.[14] Benini, in remarking that the number 515 is transcribed in Latin letters by DXV, interprets these as initials designating *Dante, Veltro di Cristo*; but this interpretation is singularly far-fetched, and moreover nothing authorizes us to suppose that Dante wanted to identify himself with this 'messenger of God'. In reality it suffices simply to change the order of the numeric letters to arrive at DVX, that is, the word *Dux*, which can be understood without further explanation;[15] and we will add that the sum of the numerals in 515 again gives the number 11.[16] This *Dux* may very well be Henry of Luxembourg, if one wishes, but it is also and by the same right any other leader chosen by the same organizations to realize the objective that they set themselves in the social order, and that Scottish Masonry still calls 'the reign of the Holy Empire'.[17]

---

that can be given of a symbolism resting on a phonetic similarity; and we will even add that in various languages the root *can* or *kan* means 'power', which is again linked to the same order of ideas.

14. The emperor as conceived by Dante is wholly comparable to the *Chakravartī* or universal monarch of the Hindus, whose essential function is to maintain peace *sarvabhaumika*, that is, extending over the whole earth; there are some parallels to be drawn between this theory of the empire and that of the Caliphate in Muḥyi 'd-Dīn.

15. We can note moreover that this *Dux* is the equivalent of the Tartar *Khan*.

16. Likewise, DIL, the first letters of the words *Diligite justitiam...*, and which are first stated separately (*Paradiso*, XVIII, 78), have the value 551, which is formed from the same figures as 515 arranged in a different order, and which also reduces to 11.

17. Certain Supreme Councils of the Scottish Rite, however, notably that of Belgium, have eliminated from their Constitutions and rituals the expression 'Holy Empire' wherever it was found. We see here the sign of a singular lack of comprehension of symbolism even in its most fundamental elements, and this shows to what degree of degeneracy certain segments of contemporary Masonry have sunk, even in the highest grades.

8

COSMIC
CYCLES

AFTER THESE OBSERVATIONS, which we believe appropriate for settling some important historical points, we arrive at what Benini calls the 'chronology' of Dante's poem. We have already recalled that Dante accomplished his journey across the worlds during Holy Week, that is to say at the time in the liturgical year that corresponds to the vernal equinox; and we have also seen that according to Aroux it was at this time that the *Cathars* performed their initiations. On the other hand, in the Masonic Rosicrucian Chapters, the commemoration of the Last Supper is celebrated on Holy Thursday, and work resumes symbolically on Friday at three o'clock in the afternoon, that is to say on the day and at the hour when Christ died. Finally, the commencement of this Holy Week in the year 1300 coincided with the full moon, and in order to complete the coincidences reported by Aroux, one could point out apropos of this that it is also at the full moon that the *Noachites* hold their meetings.

The year 1300 marks for Dante the middle of his life (he was then 35 years old), and for him it is also the mid-point of time; here again, we will quote Benini:

> Transported by an extraordinary egocentrism, Dante set his vision at the middle of the world's dur-ation—the movement of the heavens had lasted 65 centuries before him, and would extend 65 more after him—and, by a clever contrivance, had the exact anniversaries of some of the greatest events in history meet

in three kinds of astronomical years, and, in a fourth kind, the anniversary of the most important event of his own life.

What must hold our attention here above all is the calculation of the total duration of the world, or rather of the present cycle: two times 65 centuries, namely 130 centuries or 13,000 years, of which the 13 centuries that have elapsed since the beginning of the Christian era form exactly a tenth. Moreover, the number 65 is remarkable in itself since by the addition of its numerals it again comes to 11, and this number 11 is composed of 6 and 5, which are the symbolic numbers of the macrocosm and the microcosm respectively, both of which Dante derives from principial unity when he says: 'Così come raia dell'*un*, se si conosce, il *cinque* e il *sei*.'[1] Lastly, by transposing 65 into Roman numerals, as we have done for 515, we have lxv, or, with the same inversion as before, lvx, namely the word *Lux*, and this may have a connection with the Masonic era of the *True Light*.[2]

But what is more interesting is that the duration of 13,000 years is none other than the half-period of the precession of the equinoxes, exceeding the exact value by only 40 years (hence less than half a century), and thus representing an acceptable approximation, especially where this period is expressed in centuries. Indeed, the total period is in reality 25,920 years, so that half of it is 12,960 years. This half-period is the 'great year' of the Persians and the Greeks, and was sometimes estimated at 12,000 years, which is far less exact than Dante's figure of 13,000. This 'great year' was in fact regarded by the ancients as the time elapsing between two renewals of the world, which, in the history of terrestrial humanity, must doubtless be interpreted as the interval separating the great cataclysms during which entire continents disappeared (of which the last was the destruction of Atlantis). Actually, this is only a secondary cycle, which can be considered part of another more extended cycle; but by virtue of a certain law of correspondence, each of the secondary

---

1. *Paradiso*, xv, 56–57. ['. . . as *five* and *six*, if understood, ray forth from *unity*.']
2. We will add further that in Hebrew the number 65 is that of the divine name *Adonai*.

cycles reproduces, on a reduced scale, phases comparable to those of the great cycles of which it is a part. What can be said of the cyclical laws in general will therefore find its application at different degrees: historical cycles, geological cycles, and true cosmic cycles, with divisions and subdivisions that further multiply these possibilities of application. Besides, when one goes beyond the limits of the terrestrial world, there can no longer be any question of measuring the duration of a cycle by a number of years understood literally; the numbers then take on a purely symbolic value, and express proportions rather than real durations. It is no less true that in Hindu cosmology all cyclical numbers are based essentially on the period of the precession of the equinoxes, with which they have some clearly determined relationships.[3] The precessional movement is thus the fundamental phenomenon upon which the astronomical application of cyclical laws rests, and is consequently the natural point of departure for the many analogical transpositions to which these same laws might give rise. Limited space precludes our developing these considerations here, but it is remarkable that Dante adopted the same basis for his symbolic chronology; and we note here again his perfect agreement with the traditional doctrines of the East.[4]

We may ask ourselves, however, why Dante situates his vision exactly at the mid-point of the 'great year', and whether it is really necessary to speak of 'egocentrism' in this respect, or whether there are not reasons for it of another order. Let us first point out that if one selects any starting-point in time and then counts the duration

---

3. The principal of these cyclic numbers are 72, 108, and 432; it is easy to see that these are exact divisors of the number 25,920, to which they are directly linked by the geometric division of the circle; and this division itself is yet another application of cyclic numbers.

4. Besides, there is a basic accord between all traditions, whatever their differences of form; thus it is that the theory of the four ages of humanity (which relates to a more extended cycle than that of 13,000 years) is found in Greco-Roman antiquity, among the Hindus, and among the peoples of Central America as well. We find an allusion to these four ages (of gold, silver, bronze, and iron) in the figure of 'the old man of Crete' (*Inferno*, xiv, 94–120), which, moreover, is identical to the statue in Nebuchadnezzar's dream (Dan. 11); and Dante's four rivers that flow out of Hell are not without a certain analogical relationship to those of the Terrestrial Paradise; all this can be understood only by reference to cyclical laws.

of the cyclical period from this origin, one always ends up at a point that is in perfect correspondence with that from which one started, for it is this very correspondence between the elements of successive cycles that ensures their continuity. One can therefore choose the origin so as to position oneself ideally at the mid-point of such a period. This yields two equal durations, the one anterior and the other posterior, in the totality of which the full revolution of the heavens actually takes place, since all things finally find themselves in a position, not identical (to claim that would be to fall into the error of Nietzsche's 'eternal return'), but corresponding analogically to the one they had at the beginning. This can be represented geometrically in the following way: if the cycle in question is the half-period of the precession of the equinoxes, and if the entire cycle is represented by a circumference, it will suffice to trace a horizontal diameter to divide this circumference into two halves, each of which will represent a half-period the beginning and end of which correspond to the two extremities of the diameter. If we consider only the upper half-circumference, and if we trace the vertical radius, it will end at the median point corresponding to the 'mid-point of time'. The figure thus obtained is the sign $\oplus$, that is, the alchemical symbol for the mineral kingdom;[5] surmounted by a cross, it becomes the 'globe of the world', hieroglyph of the Earth and emblem of imperial power.[6] This use of the symbol in question leads one to think that for Dante it must have had a particular value; and the addition of the cross is implied in the fact that the central point where it was placed corresponded geographically to Jerusalem, which represented for him what we can call the 'spiritual pole'.[7] Furthermore, at the antipodes of Jerusalem, that is to say at the other pole, rises the Mount of Purgatory, over which shine the four stars that together form the constellation

5. This symbol is one of those that refer to the quaternary division of the circle, the analogical applications of which are almost innumerable.

6. Cf. Oswald Wirth [1860–1943], *Le Symbolisme hermétique dans ses rapports avec l'Alchimie et la Franc-Maçonnerie* [Paris: Dervy, 1995], pp19 and 70–71.

7. The symbolism of the pole plays an important role in all traditional doctrines; but in order to give a complete explanation, it would be necessary to devote to it a special study.

of the 'Southern Cross'.[8] This is the entrance to the Heavens, just as the entrance to Hell is found beneath Jerusalem; and we find depicted in this opposition the antithesis of 'Christ suffering' and 'Christ triumphant'.

At first glance it may seem astonishing that we thus draw a comparison between a chronological and a geographical symbolism; and yet this is where we wanted to arrive in order to give to the preceding remarks their real significance, for the temporal succession involved is itself only a mode of symbolic expression. Any cycle can be divided into two phases, which are, chronologically, its successive halves, and it is in this form that we have envisaged them in the first place; but in reality these two phases represent, respectively, the action of two adverse and yet complementary tendencies; and this action can obviously be simultaneous as well as successive. To place oneself at the mid-point of the cycle is therefore to place oneself at the point where these two tendencies counter-balance each other. It is, as the Islamic initiates say, 'the divine place where contrasts and antinomies are reconciled'; it is the center of the 'wheel of things', according to the Hindu expression, or the 'invariable middle' of the Far-Eastern tradition—the fixed point around which takes place the rotation of the spheres, the perpetual movement of the manifested world. Dante's journey is accomplished by following the 'spiritual axis' of the world; indeed, only from there can one view all things in permanent mode, because one is oneself exempt from change, and consequently has a view that is synthetic and total.

From a properly initiatic point of view, what we have just indicated corresponds yet again to a profound truth: the being must above all identify the center of its own individuality (represented by the heart in traditional symbolism) with the cosmic center of the state of existence to which this individuality belongs, and which it takes as a base from which to raise itself to the higher states. It is in this center that perfect equilibrium resides, an image of principial immutability in the manifested world; it is there that the axis connecting all the states projects itself, the 'divine ray' that in its ascent

---

8. *Purgatorio*, I, 22–27.

leads directly to the higher states to be attained. Each point possesses these possibilities virtually, and is so to speak a potential center, but it is necessary that it become so effectively, through a real identification, to render possible the total development of the being at the present moment. This is why, in order to raise himself to the heavens, Dante has first of all to place himself at a point that is truly the center of the terrestrial world, both according to time and space, that is to say in relation to the conditions that essentially characterize existence in this world.

Returning now to the geometric representation used earlier, we see again that the vertical radius, which runs from the surface of the earth to its center, corresponds to the first part of Dante's journey, that is, the journey through Hell. The center of the earth is the lowest point because it is toward this that the forces of gravity exert themselves from all sides; as soon as it is passed, the ascent commences, accomplished in the opposite direction and ending at the antipodes of the point of departure. To represent this second phase, the radius must then be extended beyond the center, so as to complete the vertical diameter; we then have the figure of a circle divided by a cross, namely the sign ⊕, which is the Hermetic symbol for the vegetable kingdom. Now, if one looks in a general way at the symbolic elements that play a preponderant role in the first two parts of Dante's poem, one sees in fact that they relate to the mineral and vegetable kingdoms respectively. We will not stress the obvious relation that unites the first to the interior regions of the earth, and will only recall the 'mystical trees' of Purgatory and of the Terrestrial Paradise. One might expect the correspondence to continue between the third phase and the animal kingdom,[9] but this is not so, because the limits of the terrestrial world have here been surpassed,

---

9. The Hermetic symbol of the animal kingdom is the sign ⊕, which is made up of the complete vertical diameter and only half of the horizontal diameter; this symbol is in a way the inverse of that of the mineral kingdom, what was horizontal in the one becoming vertical in the other, and vice versa. The symbol of the vegetable kingdom, where there is a kind of symmetry or equivalence between both horizontal and vertical directions, clearly represents an intermediary stage between the other two.

so that it is no longer possible to apply the same symbolism. It is at the end of the second part, that is to say while still in the Terrestrial Paradise, that we find the greatest abundance of animal symbols; it is necessary first to traverse the three kingdoms, representing the various modalities of existence in our world, before passing on to other states, where conditions are altogether different.[10]

We must still consider the points at the opposite extremities of the axis passing through the earth, namely Jerusalem and the Terrestrial Paradise. These are the vertical projections, as it were, of the two points marking the beginning and the end of the chronological cycle, which in the preceding diagram corresponded to the extremities of the horizontal diameter. If we let these latter represent their opposition according to time, and if those of the vertical diameter represent their opposition according to space, we then have an expression of the complementary roles of these two principles, the action of which is rendered, in our world, as the two conditions time and space. The vertical projection could be regarded as a projection into the 'intemporal', if we may so put it, seeing that it is accomplished along the axis whence all things are envisaged in permanent, and no longer transitory, mode; the passage from the horizontal to the vertical diameter therefore represents in reality a transmutation of succession into simultaneity.

But, one will ask, what connection exists between these two points in question and the extremities of the chronological cycle? For one point, the Terrestrial Paradise, this connection is obvious, since it is really this which corresponds to the beginning of the cycle, but for the other it must be noted that the Terrestrial Jerusalem is taken as the prefiguration of the Celestial Jerusalem described in the Apocalypse; symbolically, moreover, it is also in Jerusalem that the place of the resurrection and judgement that end the

---

10. We might point out that in certain rites the three grades of symbolic Masonry have passwords that also represent, respectively, the three kingdoms, mineral, vegetable, and animal. Furthermore, the first of these words is sometimes interpreted in a sense closely connected with the symbolism of the 'globe of the world'.

cycle are situated. The antipodal positions of these two points take on a new significance if we observe that the Celestial Jerusalem is none other than the very reconstitution of the Terrestrial Paradise, according to an analogy applied in an inverse sense.[11] At the 'beginning of time', that is to say of the present cycle, the Terrestrial Paradise was rendered inaccessible following the fall of man; the New Jerusalem must 'descend from Heaven to Earth' at the end of this same cycle to mark the re-establishment of all things in their primordial order; and one can say that it will play the same role for the future cycle that the Terrestrial Paradise does for this one. Indeed, the end of a cycle is analogous to its beginning, and coincides with the commencement of the following cycle. What was only virtual at the start of the cycle is effectively realized at its end, and immediately engenders the virtualities that will develop in their turn in the course of the future cycle. But this is a matter which we cannot pursue further without departing completely from our subject.[12] We will only add, for the sake of pointing out yet another aspect of the same symbolism, that the center of the being, to which we alluded above, is referred to in the Hindu tradition as the 'City of Brahma' (in Sanskrit *Brahmapura*), and that several texts speak of it in terms almost identical to those we find in the apocalyptic description of the Celestial Jerusalem.[13] Finally, to return to what more directly

11. The same relationship obtains between the Terrestrial Paradise and the Celestial Jerusalem as between the two Adams spoken of by Saint Paul (1 Cor. 15).

12. Concerning these remarks there are still many other questions that would be worth exploring. Why, for example, is the Terrestrial Paradise described as a garden and with a vegetable symbolism whereas the Celestial Jerusalem is described as a city and with a mineral symbolism? It is because vegetation represents the development of seeds in the sphere of vital assimilation whereas minerals represent results that are fixed definitively, 'crystallized' so to speak, at the end of the cyclical development.

13. The comparison to which these texts gives rise is even more significant when we know the relationship that connects the Lamb [*l'Agneau*] in Christian symbolism with the Vedic *Agni* (of which the vehicle, furthermore, is represented by the ram). We do not claim that there is between the words *Agnus* [Lamb] and *Ignis* [Fire] (the Latin equivalent of *Agni*) anything more than one of those phonetic similarities we alluded to above, which may very well not correspond to any

concerns Dante's journey, it is fitting to note that if the crossing of the terrestrial world ends at the beginning point of the cycle, this is an explicit allusion to the 'return to origins' that holds so important a place in all traditional doctrines, and on which, by a most remarkable coincidence, Islamic esoterism and Taoism most particularly insist. It is again a question of the restoration of the 'Edenic state', of which we have already spoken, and which must be regarded as a preliminary condition for the conquest of the superior states of the being.

The point equidistant from the two extremities just mentioned, that is to say the center of the earth, is, as we have already pointed out, the lowest point, and it corresponds also to the middle of the cosmic cycle if this cycle is envisaged chronologically, or under the aspect of succession. We can in fact divide the whole cycle into two phases, the one descending, proceeding in the direction of ever more accentuated differentiation, the other ascending, returning toward the principial state. These two phases, which the Hindu doctrine compares to those of respiration, are also to be found in the Hermetic doctrine, where they are called 'coagulation' and 'solution': by virtue of the laws of analogy, the 'Great Work' reproduces in abbreviated form the whole cosmic cycle. Here we can see the respective predominance of the opposing tendencies *tamas* and *sattva*, which we have already defined: the first is manifested in all forces of contraction and condensation, the second in all forces of expansion and dilation, and in this respect we also find a correspondence with the opposite properties of heat and cold, the first dilating bodies, while the second contracts them; and this is why the last circle of Hell is frozen. Lucifer symbolizes 'the inverse attraction of

---

linguistic relationship at all, strictly speaking, but which are not for all that accidental. What we particularly want to speak of is a certain aspect of the symbolism of fire which, in various traditional forms, is linked very closely to the idea of Love, transposed in a higher sense as Dante uses it; and in this Dante again was inspired by Saint John, to whom the Orders of Chivalry have always principally linked their doctrinal conceptions. It is fitting to note further that the Lamb is found associated both with representations of the Terrestrial Paradise and with those of the Celestial Jerusalem.

nature', that is to say the tendency toward individualization, with all the limitations inherent in it. His abode is therefore *il punto al qual si traggon d'ogni parte i pesi*,[14] or, in other words, the center of the attractive and compressive forces represented by gravity in the terrestrial world; and the latter, which attracts bodies downward (that is, toward the center of the earth), is really a manifestation of *tamas*. We note in passing that this goes against the geological hypothesis of the 'central fire', for the lowest point must be precisely the one where density and solidity are at their maximum; and on the other hand, it is no less contrary to the hypothesis put forward by some astronomers of an 'end of the world' by freezing, since that end can only be a return to indifferentiation. Besides, the last hypothesis is in contradiction to all traditional conceptions: it was not only for Heraclitus and the Stoics that the destruction of the world must coincide with its conflagration; the same affirmation is found almost everywhere, from the *Purānas* of India to the Apocalypse; and we must note again the agreement of these traditions with the Hermetic doctrine, for which fire (that element in which *sattva* predominates) is the agent of the 'renewal of nature' or of the 'final restoration'.

The center of the earth thus represents the extreme point of manifestation in the state of existence under consideration; it is a true stopping-point, from which a change of direction occurs, the preponderance passing from one to the other of the contrary tendencies. This is why an ascent or return toward the principle commences immediately following upon a descent to the bottom of Hell; and the passage from one to the other hemisphere is made by skirting the body of Lucifer in a way that leads us to think that this central point is not without certain correspondences to the Masonic mysteries of the 'Middle Chamber', where it is also a question of death and resurrection. Here again we find parallel symbolic expressions of the two complementary phases that, in initiation or in the Hermetic 'Great Work' (essentially one and the same thing), express these same universally applicable cyclical laws upon which, we believe, rests the entire construction of Dante's poem.

14. *Inferno*, XXXIV, 110–111. ['. . . the point to which all gravities are drawn.']

9

ERRORS OF
SYSTEMATIC
INTERPRETATIONS

SOME WILL PERHAPS THINK that this study raises more questions than it answers, and to tell the truth we can hardly protest such a criticism, if indeed it is a criticism, for it could only be such on the part of those who are ignorant of how greatly initiatic knowledge differs from all profane knowledge. That is why from the start we have been careful to give notice that we did not intend to offer a complete account, for the very nature of the subject precludes any such claim; moreover, in this domain everything is so tightly interconnected that it would certainly require several volumes to develop as they would warrant, the many questions to which we have alluded in the course of our work, not to mention all those we have not had occasion to consider, but to which this development, were we to undertake it, would inevitably lead.

In conclusion, so that no one misunderstand our intentions, we shall only say that the points of view we have expressed are by no means exclusive, and that there are doubtless many others one could take equally well, and from which no less important conclusions could be drawn, all these points of view complementing each other in perfect concordance within the unity of the total synthesis. It is of the very essence of initiatic symbolism that it cannot be reduced to more or less narrowly systematic formulas such as profane philosophy delights in; the role of symbols is to function as a support for conceptions of which the possibilities of extension are truly unlimited, and indeed, every expression is itself only a symbol.

One must therefore always reserve a place for the inexpressible, which, in the order of pure metaphysics, is really what matters most.

Under these circumstances it will be readily understood that our claims are limited to furnishing a point of departure for the reflection of those who, taking a genuine interest in these studies, are capable of understanding their real scope, and to pointing out for them paths of research from which we believe a special benefit could be derived. If this work has the effect of stimulating other studies along the same lines, this alone will be a far from negligible result, the more so since for us it is not a question of more or less vain erudition but of true comprehension; and it is no doubt only through such means that it will some day be possible to make our contemporaries aware of how narrow and insufficient are their customary ideas. The end we have in view is perhaps far distant, but we cannot prevent ourselves from thinking of it and striving after it, even as for our part we contribute however feebly to shedding light on an aspect of Dante's work that is far too little known.

INDEX

Made in the USA
Middletown, DE
03 December 2017